The Gift of Simplicity

Discover the Rewards of Simplifying Your Life

The Gift of Simplicity

of

Simplicity

Discover the Rewards
of Simplifying
Your Life

Joan Barclay

ISBN # 1-58721-313-3

This book is printed on acid free paper.

1stBooks Rev. – 11/3/00

Dedicated
with love and gratitude
to my parents

ACKNOWLEDGMENTS

My special thanks to Jane Comerford of Portland Community College for responding enthusiastically to the concept of my workshop, "The Gift of Simplicity," and later encouraging me to write this book expanding on the course. My appreciation to my friends and students who were excited by the ideas and wished to see them published. Thanks to my editor for his helpful suggestions, and to the staff at 1st Books for their assistance and expertise in publishing the book.

PREFACE

In early 1993, in response to the increasing complexity and pace of daily life, high consumption and mounting debts, and the growing threats to our global ecology, I created a workshop called, "The Gift of Simplicity." The enthusiastic response to this class over the years, and the continuing interest shown by people I meet, has prompted me to write this book expanding on the course. This practical and inspiring guide to a simpler life draws on my lifelong experience, as well as additional research.

Born and raised in Scotland until I was twelve, I grew up experiencing the joy of simple pleasures and learning the wisdom of staying out of debt. I carried these values and attitudes of my early years into adulthood in the U.S.A. I chose to let my values determine my priorities, and developed my own simple system for curtailing my consumption, while I saved on a regular basis. I was more inclined to spend on travel and other intangible goals instead of on many possessions.

After earning a degree in anthropology, I traveled and lived in Europe for several years, where I experienced a variety of simple lifestyles. These early experiences helped foster my lifelong appreciation for the lightness and greater freedom of living with simplicity, and the opportunity it affords for inner growth. I have lived simply whether working in the corporate world, or teaching my workshop, and continue to enjoy the rewards of a simple lifestyle.

I hope this book will guide and inspire you, too, in your journey to a simpler, more balanced and rewarding life.

CONTENTS

INTRODUCTION

A simple life is its own reward

—*George Santayana*

Like a diamond, simplicity has various facets, all contributing to the radiance of a well-balanced life. Each chapter covers a different aspect, from the philosophical foundation, to the practical suggestions and guidelines that follow. You may read the book from cover to cover, to discover how one facet contributes to the rest; or dip into it wherever you choose for inspiration and guidance over the months and years.

Most chapters end with suggested goals, as well as action steps to help you reach them. Taking these steps will lead you into a simpler life. You may eliminate some, add your own, and adjust the time frames to meet your own requirements.

Exercises throughout the book help you practice new techniques, explore different strategies, and begin taking steps to simplify your life. With patience, discipline, and commitment, you can develop your awareness, reflect on your values, become aware of your choices, and realize what brings you peace.

Learn to change your attitude toward possessions, and reduce the clutter in your life. Follow tips to help you spend wisely, and escape the burdens of debt and over-consumption. Create your own budget from forms and instructions in the appendix of the book. Find guidance and inspiration to enhance the quality of your time, and provide needed nourishment for your soul. Follow suggestions for healthful eating and simplify your diet to improve your health and sense of well-being. Finally, you'll discover that as you create more joy, peace, and balance in your personal life, you will be living more in harmony with all life, and the Earth.

How you simplify, and to what extent, will be entirely up to you. We all live in varying circumstances, with different physical and emotional needs. Our work and places of business create their own demands. We have different options depending on whether we are single, a partner in a couple, or a member of a family with children of various ages. Use this book to help create and implement a vision for your life. It will aid the busy professional searching for more balance; or people seeking ways to live within their means. It will help the individual living in retirement; and the person who is searching for a more rewarding life.

"Don't cling to the old because it made you glad once—Go on to the next: The next region, the next experience," wrote Alfred North Whitehead. Plan to take some action, make commitments, and accept responsibility for shaping the lifestyle you desire. As you develop new habits, and build on your successes, you will reap the various rewards. Take it one step at a time, beginning with those areas you feel drawn to explore. Let the rest go until you are ready to make them part of your life. Above all, value yourself enough to want to give yourself more time and more peace, and to move toward the inner completion, and true fulfillment, that nourishes your soul.

"I learned this, at least, by my experiment:" wrote Henry Thoreau of his experience in simple living at Walden Pond: "That if one advances confidently in the direction of his dreams and endeavors to live the life which he has imagined, he will meet with a success unexpected in common hours. He will put some things behind, will pass an invisible boundary; new universal, and more liberal laws will begin to establish themselves around and within him;...and he will live with the license of a higher order of beings. In proportion as he simplifies his life, the laws of the universe will appear less complex,...If you have built castles in the air, your work need not be lost; that is where they should be. Now put the foundations under them." In the pages to follow you will learn how.

CHAPTER *1*

SEARCHING FOR COMPLETION

What good is it for a man to gain the whole world, yet forfeit his soul?

—(Mark 8:36)

THE SEARCH

The hunger for something to make us complete

Most of us suffer from a pervading sense of restlessness, emptiness, or vague yearning. We hunger for something, or someone, to satisfy our longing. We yearn for the perfect partner, yet often after we find someone, continue to feel alone. With disillusionment, divorce or broken relationships often occur, and we find ourselves searching for someone once again. Children or grandchildren may alleviate our yearning, but they become independent with a path of their own, and the sense of inner emptiness resurfaces again. We seek relief in crowds and in constant activity, yet they mask, rather than relieve, our sense of inner restlessness. We acquire endless possessions, fill the silence with sound, seek fulfillment in our profession or career, and climb the ladder to success.

Chasing the 10,000 things

For many, this is the paradox of life today. We have attained the high-powered job, the beautiful home, the expensive car—sure that it will bring us happiness, and the sense of accomplishment we deserve. Instead, with success in hand, we find ourselves feeling empty and unfulfilled, and wondering why. In Buddhism, it is referred to as "Chasing the 10,000 Things." It's a search that is fruitless and endless because it's directed out there —away from the source of true fulfillment, that lies within.

We won't find completion when we are promoted, or start our own business; we won't find it when we buy a new home, or reach retirement. After each new achievement, our brief satisfaction quickly turns to ashes in our mouth. Something is missing, but what? What are we seeking so endlessly?

INNER COMPLETION

Unrest versus fulfillment

At the beginning of 1995, when a friend asked, "How are you doing?" I replied by describing how I had felt when I awoke in the wee hours a few nights before: — "I lay in bed thinking something is missing, I'm not in the right place, tossing and turning, and wondering what I should be doing with my life. You know how things feel at 3:00 o'clock in the morning!" I had exclaimed. "I feel so complete when I am here," I added with a feeling of longing, referring to our weekly inspirational gathering, which had just disbanded. "I wish I could always feel as I do when I am here."

My friend offered a few comments, concluding with the statement, "You know the answer!"

A few hours later it came to me. As I mulled over our conversation I recalled that while telling him how I had felt a few nights before, I really had no such questions during our interchange. Somehow, I had discounted that at the time, thinking my feelings at 3:00 a.m. reflected my true inner state. I still retained the sense of inner completion engendered at our gathering that morning; and I was conscious of the contrast between the way I now felt with my feelings of several nights before. My sense of unrest, and lack of fulfillment, had vanished like dreams at the moment of waking.

As I contemplated this contrast, I recalled having a meaningful realization a few years earlier. I had experienced the same sense of inner wholeness while I walked through a stately mansion, built almost 100 years before. It was now a museum, surrounded by many acres of beautiful gardens, lawns and trees, and open to the public. Standing half-way up the gracefully curving, white marble staircase, I had looked around me; admiring the original art, beautiful antique decor, and elegant architecture of this once luxurious home. Suddenly I had been filled with a sense of inner completion and peace. I remembered it clearly. I had paused there, imbued with utter contentment, and had known with certainty that as long as I had that feeling, it would not matter where I lived. Lingering there, I had imagined myself in various surroundings—from a simple cabin, to owning that beautiful mansion. All had felt acceptable and right. At the same time, I had known that without that realization of inner completion, even living in that elegant home would not have satisfied me.

Inner completion

Then I realized, as I had before in the mansion, that it would not matter whether I had a simple role in life, or a world changing mission, after experiencing that sense of inner completion. At the same time, I knew that without that inner realization, neither lofty achievements, nor endlessly seeking for the right place would satisfy me.

This, I thought, is what we are really seeking: It's that sense of inner wholeness, inner connection and expanded awareness. It's what some call experiencing the presence of God, and others refer to as our "true nature." This alone brings true fulfillment, peace and joy, no matter what we possess, or what we do and achieve. With this sense of inner completion, we feel free and fully alive, ready to respond as life unfolds from moment to moment.

"How can I experience that sense of inner fulfillment?" you may ask. "What must I do to find this inner peace?" Perhaps you sense that this is the answer you are seeking, but how—how can you attain it?

We have inadvertently starved our souls

Caught up in our lives of constant striving, ceaseless activity, countless possessions, and background noise, we have inadvertently starved our souls. "What good is it for a man to gain the whole world, yet forfeit his soul?" Jesus asked (Mark 8:36). With all our efforts to satisfy our inner hunger directed out there, we may have gained the world, but have cut ourselves off from the inner peace and heightened awareness that nourish our soul.

With a life of constant action, we strive to alleviate our inner yearning. "If I don't keep constantly busy," we sometimes believe, "I will be depressed," and so we eliminate the peaceful times we need. Bombarded with sound from morning 'til night, we muffle our gnawing hunger and mental turmoil. The television, radio, or stereo provides a background to our conversation, thoughts, and activities; but deprives us of the silence we require. In the Western world, we often equate noise and activity with reality, yet both can be counterproductive to the peace and tranquillity that nourish the soul. As Wayne Muller says, "The danger of all our obligations is

3

that we lose touch with our talents and intuitions and become deaf to our inner wisdom. We can lose the capacity to appreciate the quiet moments that may bring us peace, beauty or joy."

Create time and space for solitude and silence

Create some time and space each day for solitude and silence. You may find it in the natural world and garden, in pursuit of a hobby or craft, as you perform simple tasks and activities, or in silent meditation. When we foster inner silence, and experience our true nature, we discover true contentment.

With inner contentment, we lose the need for constant action, and endless acquisitions to relieve our restless longing. We will begin to reduce the clutter in our space, time and mind. Our desire for the distractions of noise and crowds will diminish.

As we respond to life with full awareness, alert to the choices, opportunities, and inspiration of each moment, we will find that other things are added according to our need.

You may have experienced the sense of inner completion in a rare transcendent hour. You can also rest in inner stillness, and live with clear and expanded awareness, to experience inner wholeness. In this unfolding process lies fulfillment, peace, and growth.

"Through silence, solitary practice, and simple living, we begin to fill the empty reservoir." —David A. Cooper.

CHAPTER *2*

DEVELOPING YOUR AWARENESS

...the surest way to live one's live to the full,...is to cultivate the habit of living in the present
—Florence Barclay

"I find the surest way to live one's life to the full, accomplishing the maximum amount of work with the minimum amount of strain, is to cultivate the habit of living in the present; giving the whole mind to the scene, the subject, the person of the moment." In this quotation from *The Mistress of Shenstone*, a novel written in 1910, Dr. Brand is responding to a friend who, although delighted that he is spending time with her, has been protesting that he has patients who need his time far more. He concludes his remark by saying, "Therefore, with your leave, we will dismiss my patients, past and future, and enjoy, to the full, this unexpected tête à tête."

Pause and consider how much richer, more relaxing, productive, and fulfilling your life would be if you followed this precept. You could lose your feelings of frenzy, haste, frustration over lack of time, turmoil, emptiness, and sense of isolation. "Impossible," you say, "I have too many responsibilities, too much to think about, too many activities." Yet the wisdom in this quotation forms the basis of a balanced, simple life.

When we divide our attention between the person before us, our ever-changing inner dialogue with its multiplicity of concerns, and whatever else is happening around us, is it any wonder we feel harried and harassed? We experience nothing fully, and are less productive, connected, and fulfilled. Life is indeed a blur.

The wandering of your mind

The next three exercises will help you observe the workings of your mind. They are subtly different, each building on those that precede it. You may wish to spread the practice sessions over several days or weeks, returning to them to improve your experience. Now take a few minutes to observe the extent of your inner dialogue, by performing Exercise 2–1. The easiest way to accomplish that is to spend a few minutes seeking inner silence.

Exercise 2–1   Maintain inner silence

Sit in a comfortable position with your back straight, and your feet flat on the floor. Close your eyes, or look at the floor three feet in front of you. Now maintain inner silence for five minutes. Try to make this silence complete by remaining physically and mentally still. At the end of five minutes, think about your experience. How did you try to achieve inner silence? Were you successful? How did you feel?

You probably discovered that it was difficult to still the constant churning of your mind. Did it surprise you to observe this continuous stream of thought? We are usually so immersed in our inner dialogue, that we are completely unaware of its flow. Now take another two minutes to perform Exercise 2–2, and this time deliberately notice your thoughts.

Exercise 2–2   Watch the wandering of your mind

Sit comfortably, back straight, feet flat on the floor, and eyes closed or looking at the floor. For the next two minutes watch the wandering of your mind. Don't judge what you observe; just be aware of it.

Were you able to simply witness your flow of thought without becoming immersed in it? If you were, it was because a small amount of inner silence allowed you to observe your inner dialogue. Try expanding on that silence. Take five more minutes to perform Exercise 2–3.

Exercise 2–3   Experience inner silence

Sit comfortably, back straight, feet flat on the floor, and eyes closed or looking at the floor. Now try to maintain inner silence for five minutes. Were you successful? What did you observe? What thoughts, sensations and feelings did you notice?

If you were able to sit in inner silence, you may have noticed the sounds around you, or different sensations in your body. Perhaps you realized that you had been lost in thought for some of the time. The important point is that you probably became increasingly aware.

If you are willing to make the effort, you can continue to develop your awareness. Your experience of inner silence will gradually deepen, giving you a greater understanding of the working of your mind, and a clearer understanding of yourself. In addition, as you become increasingly aware, you will bring yourself completely into the present moment.

Focusing on our senses brings us into the present

We can cultivate the habit of living in the present by focusing our awareness on our sensory experiences. Take a few minutes now to bring yourself into the present, by eating a raisin with all of your attention. (If you are tempted to skip exercise 2-4 because you believe you know how the raisin will taste, please reconsider. It will reveal far more than you realize, and will enhance your understanding of the ideas that follow.)

Exercise 2–4   Eating a raisin with awareness

Get a raisin, or another small piece of food with concentrated flavor, from your cupboard. Close your eyes, put the raisin in your mouth, and slowly start to chew. Chew the raisin with complete attention until it dissolves and you swallow it. Think about this experience and what you observed.

What did you notice about the taste of the raisin? Was it sweeter than any you have eaten before? Were you surprised at how long it took to dissolve? Did you observe the movement of your tongue, your teeth, your jaws? Were you aware of the sound of your chewing? Did you notice anything else?

You may not have realized that as you focused on eating the raisin, your mind became quieter. As your mind became quieter, you experienced a small degree of inner peace, and your muscles began to relax.

When we become aware of our sensory experiences—the sounds around us, the rise and fall of our breath, the taste of our food, the feel of the car's steering wheel in our hands—we bring ourselves into the present moment, and feel more alive. Practice bringing yourself into the present moment, by watching the rise and fall of your breath in Exercise 2–5.

> **Exercise 2–5   Watch the rise and fall of your breath**
>
> Sit comfortably. back straight, feet flat on the floor, and eyes closed or looking at the floor. Start by exhaling, then take a deep breath, inhaling all the way down into your abdomen. Now slowly let it out. Repeat three times. This will help to center you, and silence your mind. As thoughts arise, have no interest in them; simply let them dissolve and continue to watch the rise and fall of your breath. If you realize that you have been lost in thought, gently return your awareness to your breath.   At the end of ten minutes, stop and think about your experience.

How did this experience compare with your attempt to silence your mind in Exercise 2–1? Were you more successful with Exercise 2–5? Do you feel more at peace and more relaxed?

Our perpetual inner dialogue

As you will observe through these exercises, far from being present, we are usually preoccupied and distracted, either oblivious to, or only vaguely conscious of, the experience of the moment. Most of us live in our heads, lost in our thoughts and fantasies of the past or future. We spend the minutes and hours of our days rehashing old grievances, regretting past mistakes, reliving our experiences, anticipating upcoming pleasures, and fearing what may come. Whether taking a walk, driving our car, performing a task, or anything else, our minds are engaged in this perpetual inner dialogue.

We could say our thoughts resemble the swarm of small flies I observed one day in a sunlit glade. Each one circled in its own tiny orbit, mingling with the circular paths of other small flies nearby. Some made brief solitary darts away from the general milieu, only to quickly return to it once again. Around and around they went, just like our thoughts, repeating the circuits over and over again.   Think how we miss the freshness of the present moment, when we spend our days engrossed in thoughts and emotions concerning events from the past.

Many of us often feel bored and empty. When we are fully present and attentive to our sensory experiences, however, almost everything we do becomes more vivid and enhances our feeling of being alive.

Our hunting and gathering ancestors

Consider our hunting and gathering ancestors, who inhabited the world over eleven thousand years ago. How alert and aware the men had to be when they hunted for game with which to feed and clothe their families. They listened for every sound, and followed tracks and other clues, while keeping a cautious lookout for any hint of danger. Their lives depended on their acute awareness in the moment. Vigorously active, they traveled and hunted together, dependent upon one another for strength and survival. They gave their whole minds to the scene and activity of the moment, and you can be certain that they felt exceedingly alive.

The women had to be just as aware while they searched for roots and berries. They made clothes from skins and fibers, pounded seeds, prepared food, and kept an eye on the children. They lived and worked together, alert in their senses, and part of the natural world. You can be sure that they, too, felt fully alive.

In spite of the technological progress made since prehistoric times, physiologically we are still the same. We live in a highly technical world, with brains and bodies adapted to the stone age. Our natures crave involvement with life through our presence in the moment, and our focused awareness on our sensory experiences. Our bodies, designed for action and mobility, function best when we make some form of physical activity a part of our day. Our longing for community, and interest in people around us, evolved from adaptations that enhanced survival in prehistoric times.

Inherently part of the natural world, we are nourished by contact with nature, whether by taking a walk in a sunlit wood, or buying a hyacinth for our soul. We cannot ignore our innate physiological, psychological and sociological needs, and expect to feel nurtured and vibrantly alive.

Today, we are hurried and distracted, preoccupied and separate, too overloaded with our numerous activities to take time to notice the moments of our life. We are a civilization of watchers, who often live vicariously through the television programs, movies, and images on computer screens that fill our days. We watch instead of moving, and miss the many benefits that exercise bestows. We watch without relating, and lose the opportunity to build community. We watch instead of living with presence and awareness, and forfeit the little joys that could enhance every day. We seem to have come full circle, and are hunting once again; this time for that elusive feeling of being connected and fully alive.

This moment is precious

Henry Thoreau wrote almost one hundred and fifty years ago, "I went to the woods because I wished to live deliberately, to front only the essential facts of life,…and not, when I came to die, discover that I had not lived. I didn't want to live what is not life, living is so dear, nor did I wish to practice resignation." Today, as a civilization of watchers, we often "live what is not life," and as a consequence, "practice resignation." Yes, "living is so dear," and with each lost opportunity to be present and aware, we may eventually "discover that we have not lived." As Jon Kabat Zinn says, "You have to come to the realization that this moment is precious. The little things and the little moments are not little—they are life."

Moments on a Greek Island

The closer we come to living "with the essential facts of life," the easier it becomes to experience joy in the "little things and the little moments." I learned this after graduation from college, when a friend and I spent three idyllic summer months on the Greek Island of Kos. Lying close to the Turkish mainland, the island was relatively untouched by tourism at that time. Our life there was spontaneous and carefree. We were living in the moment and in touch with the natural world.

We wore bikinis beneath simple cotton blouses and skirts, which I had sewn by hand. With rented bicycles for transportation, we stayed fit, and in contact with life all around us. Our home, a tiny whitewashed, stone cottage, included a patio, large garden, and orchard. It was located one mile from the town of Kos. Without electricity or gas that far from town, we cooked our simple meals on a small Bunsen burner flame. One saucepan, one frying pan, two plates, two cups, and two knives, forks and spoons completed our kitchenware. Our kitchen, a small, plain room, contained just one table. The large washtub and running water were outside, under the grape arbor, beside the cottage. The plumbed toilet was housed in its own small structure, complete with resident frogs. We showered back in the orchard, under a garden hose. Our bedroom, above the kitchen, contained two simple cot beds, and two straight-backed wooden chairs. We had all that we required on this sunlit island.

"What in the world did you do on a Greek Island for three months?" people asked in amazement after our return to Athens. "After all, most people tour much of Europe in only three weeks!"

"We just lived," we replied.

On our final day on the island, with the experience fresh in my mind, I wrote the following simple description of "the little things and the little moments" that had been our life that summer.

- Bicycle rides, often against strong headwinds, along the Zephyrus Road, or on the way to Marmari.

- Wonderful hours on the beaches: running the golden sands of Tigaki, Marmari, and Kardamana; basking in the brilliant sun; dipping into the sparkling sea. What freedom, such exhilaration, what happiness!

- Wildflowers everywhere: white daisies, orange poppies, purple flowers, and blue ones.

- Pink roses cascading over the arbor, framing our white gate.

- Candlelight in the bedroom, with wildflowers filling the basket bottle under the white lace curtain.

- Meals in our kitchen; shish kebab on the patio.

- Chickens scratching in our yard and in the orchard, with its olives, figs, peaches and grapes.

- Donkeys passing our window at dawn, and returning at dusk: the clip, clop of their hooves, and the "hmmm, hmmm" of their owners. There were men on them, women on them, and sometimes children, too. A few were carrying baskets; others were laden with hay.

- Cows being led to the fields; pulled and prodded by laughing boys.

- Windmills, prickly pear cactus, tiny white houses, and churches, scattered along the roads.

- Greetings from the children, the men, and the women, as we passed on foot or bicycle: "Herete! Kalimera! Yasoo! Poo Pate? Do you speak English?"

- Cafes filled with laughing men; many tossing their "worry beads."

- Almost daily bicycle rides into the town of Kos, with a stop at the open-air marketplace to buy fresh produce for the day.

- Thick, sweet, Greek coffee; delicate pastries; tart, creamy yogurt, savored in our favorite cafes at the marketplace, on the waterfront, or beside a country road.

This was Kos—my island home—where I often felt deep peace.

Experience life afresh to enhance the feeling of being alive

It's a joy to think of the simple delights of a Greek Island, isn't it? It's an experience I continue to treasure. Yet, as Marcel Proust said, "The real voyage of discovery consists not in seeking new landscapes, but in having new eyes." When we are present in the moment, alert in all of our senses, and see things as if for the first time, we have new eyes. We experience life afresh, and enhance our feeling of being alive. Embark on your own voyage of discovery, and savor "the little things and little moments" of your life:

- Stop to inhale the fragrant rose in the garden, when you pass by.
- Relish the pungent aroma of damp earth, in the early morning, after a night of rain.
- Delight in the hum of the bumble bee that buzzes past your ear.
- Thrill to the power, in the sight, and sound of crashing surf as it sweeps ashore.
- Look into the eyes of your loved ones, while you listen to their words.

These images, scents, and sounds are so elemental, and reassuring. They unite us with the natural world, bring us into the present, and give us a sense of connection and of peace.

Absorption in our activities creates inner peace

Consider the other moments in your life. Remember the times when absorbed in a favorite activity or deeply engrossed in a task you enjoyed, you lost track of time? I always delight in flower arranging. As I work on a design, I enter a timeless, peaceful state. I become so absorbed in creating balance and harmony, that my mind becomes silent. I stop fretting, rehashing, anticipating or judging. I complete the arrangement feeling serene and refreshed.

Reflect now on some of your favorite pastimes, and the pleasure they bring you, by completing Exercise 2–6.

Exercise 2–6   Recall your favorite pastimes

Recall some of your favorite pastimes. Create a list of those where you become so engrossed that you lose track of time.   How do you feel during and after these activities? Do you feel more at peace, more relaxed, or more alive?

Did you think of hours you spend in the natural world: planting or weeding your garden, rambling in the woods, strolling on the beach, hiking in the mountains? Did you recall being engaged in a creative pursuit or hobby: making pottery or woodworking, sewing or weaving, cooking for pleasure, taking photographs, arranging your stamp collection? Did you consider participating in your favorite sports, or moments at play with your child or pet?

Now turn your attention to the rest of your day. We can extend to some of our daily tasks and activities the peace, connection and relaxation we enjoy from our absorption in these pleasurable pursuits. At first it may be difficult to maintain your focus for more than a moment or two, before you are lost in your thoughts once again. As you will discover, however, your focus improves with practice. Even momentary respites add refreshment to your day. When you realize you have been distracted while attempting to focus on one of your tasks, just gently return your awareness to your activity once again. Try beginning with the simple action of walking, as you practice Exercise 2–7.

Exercise 2–7   Walk with awareness

Practice conscious walking whenever you think of it. You can do this on the nature trail, the beach, or city sidewalk. Become aware of the feel of the ground under your feet. Play a game with yourself, by deciding you'll be conscious of the ground for the next ten steps. Then add ten more steps, and so on, for as long as you can maintain your awareness. When you realize your mind has wandered, return your attention to the feel of the ground under your feet.

A walk with focused awareness will clarify your mind, provide instant refreshment, and enhance your enjoyment of the other sights and sounds around you. Bird songs, the movement of trees, details of their bark, and the sparkle of sunlight on their leaves and needles spring into view. When our mind is clear, we create an inner silence that allows the entrance of creative thoughts and insights. As Locke wrote in a letter in 1699, "The thoughts that come often unsought, and as it were, drop into the mind, are commonly the most valuable of any we have."

After you have experience in walking with awareness, try expanding your practice to simple daily tasks. Prepare a pot of coffee or tea with focused attention, or wash a few dishes by hand, dust the furniture, or some other activity of your choice. Even the act of driving your car can become a part of your practice. Begin by performing Exercise 2–8.

Exercise 2–8   Consciously prepare a cup of coffee or tea

Prepare a cup of coffee or tea. Notice the feel of the cup in your hands; observe its shape and pattern. Watch and listen to the flow of the water into the cup. Observe the curling wisp of steam as it rises in the air. Sit down and drink it with conscious pleasure. Relish the peace and relaxation of these minutes.

Decide to perform a simple task with full attention for the count of ten. Then add another ten, and continue to do so for as long as you can maintain your focus. As with any new endeavor, you will improve with practice and will learn to be conscious for longer periods of time. With persistence, you'll experience more inner peace, serenity and relaxation in the little moments of your day.

Lack of awareness can cause frustration

Think of some of the frustrations we experience in a day: misplaced keys, gloves, or an important letter; misunderstood instructions, or a missed meeting. How scattered and anxious we feel.

Our own busyness and preoccupation causes most of these frustrations. It's a vicious cycle, one leading to the other. When we are too busy, preoccupied and distracted, we're oblivious to, or only minimally aware of our actions. We don't know where we placed important items; and we have to spend precious time trying to find them again. We may miss appointments, misunderstand instructions, and lose opportunities for connection with another. You can see why as we heighten our awareness, we "accomplish the maximum amount of work with the minimum amount of strain" —(Florence Barclay).

When we have accidents, major or minor, they are often due to our preoccupation and lack of focus on our tasks or activities. I know I have suffered a few injuries as a result of too much inner chatter and absent-minded action. The pain and inconvenience we suffer from these mishaps, often force us to slow our pace, and move with heightened awareness.

Increased awareness leads to inner change

As we continue in our efforts to become more focused and aware, we will experience more silence in our minds. With more inner clarity, our own internal dialogue will become part of our awareness. "Know Thyself," Socrates declared, and with non-judgmental observation, we will begin to know ourselves. This will subtly and effortlessly lead to inner change.

A few years ago, after a period of prolonged inner peace, I had sufficient mental clarity to observe my own reaction to an unexpected occurrence. I had returned to my residence, expecting to find everything clean and orderly after a party which had been held on the premises. Instead I found the kitchen in total disarray. A silent part of my mind witnessed my inner calm dissolve in anger. Although I was alone, I was indignant. As I prepared my meal amid the disorder, I inwardly fumed. As the minutes ticked past, the silent part of my mind observed that with every churning thought, I fueled my anger. With continued observation, my inner chatter began to seem increasingly self-indulgent. The very act of awareness began to lead to change.

I realized that after my initial surprise and dismay, I was apparently choosing to feel angry. How dare they be so inconsiderate, my injured self declared. I eventually grew weary of the turmoil. I realized that it was disturbing no one but myself, and decided I could change my thoughts. After all, there was probably an explanation for the disarray. Whatever the reason, I realized that I could choose how I would interpret the situation. I deliberately turned my attention to my sensory experiences of that moment, by plunging my hands into the soapy dishwater, and becoming aware of its silky smoothness against my skin. I washed the dishes with focused awareness, and in minutes returned to my former state of calm and peace.

It was illuminating to consciously witness my inner dialogue quickly take me from a state of inner peace, to anger and distress. Then to observe that by silencing my thoughts through focused awareness in the present, I soon returned to inner calm. It is enlightening to realize that depending on our inner dialogue, the identical event, person, or place can leave us feeling overwhelmed, frustrated, angry; or conversely, unperturbed and calm. Normally, we are so immersed in our thoughts, judgments, and emotional turmoil over people, circumstances and events, that we are oblivious to our own contribution to the feelings and actions which are aroused.

While we may initially experience anger, annoyance, or distress over an incident, or misunderstanding; with increasing awareness we can choose not to fuel it with a flow of additional dialogue. If we find ourselves embroiled in thoughts of fear, anger or dismay, it will be revealing to observe the effects of our own mental turmoil on our emotions. Try performing Exercise 2–9 the next time you find yourself becoming agitated.

Exercise 2–9   Stop your disturbing inner dialogue

The next time you find yourself worrying or fretting over some incident or person, deliberately choose to stop your thoughts. If you find this too difficult, try turning your attention to your sensory experiences in the moment: Become aware of the actions of your hands, or the feel of the ground under your feet; the taste of your food, or the rise and fall of your breath. Stay with it, and keep returning to it each time you realize that you have resumed your disturbing inner dialogue.

What did you discover from this exercise? Were you successful in silencing your thoughts? Did you become more peaceful and relaxed?

Awareness gives the power of choice

In the previous example, I later realized that it was my own *expectations,* and *interpretation* of the situation, which had disturbed my inner peace. The condition of the kitchen was not as I expected it to be, and I interpreted its disorder as inconsideration for me. If I had returned and had accepted the room as it was without judgment; then had cleared some space to prepare my meal, I would have remained calm. If I had felt initial surprise and annoyance, but had been aware enough to consciously choose to let it pass without additional inner dialogue, I could have maintained my inner peace. Simple awareness brings the power of choice, and subtly and effortlessly leads to change.

Through awareness, I observed the effect of my inner dialogue on my emotions, and eventually realized I could make a different choice. I was pleased to observe that a few weeks later, when I again encountered the same situation, I consciously responded without inner torment, and calmly cleared some space to prepare my meal. I had spared myself considerable emotional turmoil and misspent energy, and continued to enjoy inner tranquillity.

Think how this approach could reduce the frenzy, and the anguish, in our day. When we are aware, we can draw on the lessons we have learned, and the insights we have gained to grow, and to enhance the quality of our lives. When we are attentive to the choices, and the potential of each moment, we will eventually discover that "when a person finds no peace within himself, it is useless to seek it elsewhere"—(Anonymous).

Summary

We experience life more fully and heighten our feelings of being alive, when we cultivate the habit of living in the present. Instead, preoccupied and distracted, we are either oblivious to, or only partly conscious of, the scene before us. We experience nothing fully, and feel harried and harassed; frustrated by the mishaps and diminished productivity in our day.

When we become fully aware of our sensory experiences, how vividly we experience those moments in our day. When we are absorbed in a favorite pastime, or a simple daily task or activity, our mind becomes quieter; we experience a degree of inner peace, and our muscles begin to relax.

With greater inner clarity, we become aware of our own internal dialogue and gain a clearer understanding of ourselves. This subtly, and almost effortlessly, leads to inner change. With developing awareness, we can live with more intention, conscious of the choices and opportunities in each day. We will experience more peace, and greater joy in the everyday moments of our lives.

DEVELOPING YOUR AWARENESS

GOALS

Goal: To cultivate the habit of living in the present

Action:
a) Become aware of my sensory experiences
b) Practice mindful eating, and mindful walking
c) Perform simple tasks with focus and awareness

Goal: To experience more peace

Action:
a) Be conscious of my sensory experiences
b) Practice silencing my internal dialogue

Goal: To enhance the feeling of being alive

Action:
a) Be conscious of my sensory experiences
b) Be physically active
c) Have contact with nature
d) Savor all the moments of life

Goal: To experience less frustration and inconvenience

Action:
a) Bring full awareness to my actions
b) Be fully present in interactions with others

Goal: To live with more intention

Action:
a) Be conscious of the choices that I make
b) Be conscious of my reactions, interpretations and judgments
c) Choose to stop my inner dialogue when it is detrimental and judgmental by:
   - Silencing my mind
   - Changing my thoughts
   - Focusing on my sensory experiences

CHAPTER *3*

CHANGING YOUR ATTITUDE TOWARD POSSESSIONS

He who is plentiously provided for from within, needs but little from without.
—Von Goethe

How would we live without our numerous belongings? Begin this chapter by taking a minute to perform Exercise 3–1 and contemplate how you would feel without your many possessions.

Exercise 3–1   How would you feel without your possessions?

Close your eyes and imagine that all of your possessions are gone. You have only the clothes you are wearing, with enough money to eat a few meals in a restaurant, and to spend the night in a motel.   Don't worry about what you will have to do, how you will live, or care for your family or pets; just think about how it feels to be without your many possessions. Dwell on this for a minute. How do you feel?

Did you feel anxious, lost, relieved, frightened, incomplete, insecure, or liberated?

We need not identify with our possessions

Would you really be any different without your possessions? Think about your reply. We enter and leave this world with nothing, but in the interim accumulate an ever-expanding array of belongings. Each of us has a collection of well-loved, meaningful, sentimental and essential possessions: our favorite piece of furniture, the books we have read and enjoyed, our mother's china, and so on. We identify with our possessions, and most of us find it difficult to part with our precious belongings.

An acquaintance described her sister's experience following a natural disaster. "She lived in San Francisco," my acquaintance explained, "where she owned a beautiful home containing a million-dollar collection of carefully chosen, and well-loved elegant furnishings, crafts and art collected from around the world. All of this changed on October 17, 1989, when the 6.9 earthquake struck San Francisco. After the ground stopped shaking, her house was filled with rubble one foot deep. Everything had been destroyed. After she recovered from her own aftershock, her attitude toward her possessions radically changed. She now feels very detached from her belongings, and as a consequence, feels much freer."

While our possessions may feel like a part of us, we need not derive our sense of worth from what we own and acquire. If we believe the expensive car, the beautiful house or the designer labels are defining us, then we will be in bondage to the things that we possess. The same will be true if we allow others to define us by what we own, and think we must live up to their expectations in order to feel worthwhile.

If we believe that we will alleviate our inner yearning when we have a larger home, the latest in new technology, or anything else, we will always be seeking the next thing that will make us happy. It is a quest that is endless, however, because we are seeking the solution in forms outside ourselves. Until we experience our own inner wholeness, with or without our possessions, we will continue to feel that sense of longing. The answer is not to continue acquiring more, tying ourselves to a growing number of possessions, and the burden of never-ending debt. Rather it lies in expanding our awareness, and developing the inner riches that nourish our soul.

Peace Pilgrim experienced inner wholeness

Some of you may have heard of Peace Pilgrim. I had the privilege of seeing her, and hearing her speak about a year before her death in July 1981. For the last twenty-eight years of her life, she did not own anything but her simple navy blue outfit: a hip-length tunic with pockets sewn around the bottom, worn over her long-sleeved blouse and slacks. She was penniless, and had vowed to "remain a wanderer until mankind has learned the way of peace, walking until I am given shelter, and fasting until I am given food." She donated to charity all money, or material items that she received, apart from the little she used for postage to answer the letters of people who wrote. A friend forwarded her mail to her, and all she carried in the pockets of her tunic were a few of those letters, and a comb and toothbrush. She walked over 25,000 miles for peace, crossing the United States seven times.

Peace Pilgrim was in perfect health, and so filled with joy and boundless energy, she appeared to float when I saw her on the stage. It reminded me of the televised images of the astronauts when they walked on the moon. She was always conscious of inner wholeness.

"The simplification of life is one of the steps to inner peace," Peace Pilgrim said. "A persistent simplifying will create an inner and outer well-being that places harmony in one's life. For me this began with a discovery of the meaninglessness of possessions beyond my actual and immediate needs."

Living the good life

Our basic needs are so simple, yet we accumulate many possessions far beyond our requirements for survival, aesthetics and growth. This is what our culture and the media promote as the "good life." Our economy and society are built on constant consumption, with an endless array of newer and better products designed, produced, and marketed to feed our hunger. Capitalizing on our inner dissatisfaction and lack of fulfillment, we are encouraged to spend to the limit of our credit to acquire them. Endless consumption is the goal, but at what cost to us, and to the planet! If we are obsessed with the pursuit of the "good life," we will miss the elusive happiness we seek.

Enough is as good as a feast

While I was visiting my relatives in Scotland a number of years ago, my aunt turned to me one day as we prepared our noon meal and quoted, "Enough is as good as a feast, Joan, enough is as good as a feast." What could be truer? It is a phrase that has stayed with me through the years.

I love the freedom of simplicity. I also appreciate beautiful things, but we can enjoy so much that is artistic, beautiful and picturesque without having the need, or the desire, to possess it. When we have enough, how freeing it is to simply delight in the rest, whether it is in a museum, a store, someone else's home, or elsewhere. We don't have to own the property to enjoy the view. We can turn a deaf ear to the siren's song that this product or that will bring us love, beauty, or fulfillment, if we just owned it.

Do you really need it?

When you think about buying something, stop and ask yourself if you really need it. I have used this simple technique to successfully curtail my consumption and number of possessions throughout my adult life. The answer is almost always, NO. I ask myself this question almost unconsciously, no matter what the cost, or even if the item is free. Why add something else you must handle and care for, unless you really need it, or know it will add true pleasure to your life? Even if the answer is YES, think about it for a week or a month, or longer. (We will discuss this concept further in Chapter 5 under the subheading, "Practice Delaying Gratification.") This ends impulse shopping, as well as many other unnecessary purchases, and helps to reduce your consumption, and the clutter in your life. Begin this practice with Exercise 3–2.

Exercise 3–2   Do you really need it?

Whenever you are tempted to buy, ask yourself if you really need it. If the answer is NO, make an effort to forego the purchase. Even if the answer is YES, postpone it for a week, or longer, then reconsider.

Simplicity is a choice

Living with simplicity, and curtailing our consumption is not living in poverty. Rather it is an attitude and a choice. We could compare it to our decision to take a camping trip, where we are "living with only the essential facts of life and in touch with the natural world"—enjoying the utter simplicity and sense of renewal that it brings. When we go camping we are not living in poverty; nor are we when we choose a life of simplicity.

The desire to simplify may start with the cry of, "Enough!" or the question, "What is this hectic lifestyle all about?" It may arise from the longing for more time to develop our inner lives, or it may be the outer expression of inner growth. Whatever the impetus, it is a choice, and the recognition that a life of endless striving and constant accumulation does not satisfy.

As we develop our awareness, and begin to experience a growing sense of our own inner completion, increasingly we will discover that our possessions are the "added things" in our lives.

Summary

In our headlong pursuit of the "good life," we often jeopardize the very happiness we seek. In a society geared for constant consumption, the "good life" is often achieved at high cost to us, and to the planet. Our basic needs are so simple, but we accumulate possessions far beyond our requirements for survival, aesthetics and growth. When we realize that "enough is as good as a feast," we can enjoy the rest without the need, or the desire to possess. By asking ourselves if we really need it, whenever we are tempted to buy, or are offered something for free, we can reduce our consumption, and eliminate the clutter in our lives.

The decision to simplify is a choice, reflected in our changing attitudes toward possessions. It can begin with the realization that our possessions do not define us, nor can they alleviate our inner yearning. It can culminate in the realization that a life of constant striving and endless accumulation does not satisfy. When we are in touch with our inner completion, we will eventually discover that our possessions are the "added things" in our lives.

CHANGING YOUR ATTITUDE TOWARD POSSESSIONS

GOALS

Short Term: 1 – 3 months

Goal: To become a conscious shopper

> **Action:** a) Ask myself if I really need it
>
> b) Postpone a purchase for a week, a month, or longer
>
> c) Reconsider making the purchase after postponement

Intermediate: 3 – 6 months

Goal: To surrender the need to possess

> **Action:** a) Enjoy without having the need or desire to own
>
> b) Feel detached toward the media and the ads
>
> c) Realize my possessions don't define me
>
> d) Recognize possessions won't satisfy my inner longing

Long Term: 6 months – 1 year

Goal: To feel an increased sense of freedom

> **Action:** a) Relinquish the need to always have more
>
> b) Escape from the burden of too many possessions
>
> c) Stop defining myself by my possessions

CHAPTER *4*

CREATING SIMPLICITY IN YOUR LIVING SPACE

Home is the sacred refuge of our life

—*Dryden*

We feel a sense of tranquillity in an uncluttered room that is furnished simply, and enhanced with fresh flowers and some well chosen accessories.

How do you feel about your home? Clarify what makes you comfortable by answering the questions in Exercise 4–1.

Exercise 4–1 How do you feel about your home?

What makes you feel comfortable and nurtured at home? Do you like a lot of natural light and sunlight? Do you favor open, airy space? Do you enjoy a feeling of seclusion and privacy? Is your house too large? Is it too small? Is it just right? Is it cluttered or overcrowded?

Do you have more house than you need?

If your house is larger than you require, you have higher rent or mortgage payments, more property taxes, larger utility bills, and increased insurance premiums. You will have to spend more time cleaning and maintaining the house, and caring for all of your possessions.

Peace Pilgrim speaks of a woman who was getting on in years, and who was always complaining about how hard she had to work. "Why do you work so much," Peace Pilgrim asked, "when you have only yourself to support?" "Because I have to pay rent on a five-room house," was the sad reply. "But why do you need so much space?" Peace Pilgrim inquired. "Well," the lady responded, " I have furniture for a five-room house."

"Don't have more house than you need," Peace Pilgrim said, "unnecessary possessions are unnecessary burdens. If you have them, you have to take care of them." In addition, you have to pay for the privilege, either in higher rent or house payments, or for the use of a storage locker.

The lure of storage lockers

We have numerous reasons for retaining our extra possessions. You may know someone who has moved from a large home to a smaller one, but found it impossible to part with any of their belongings. Instead, they put them into a storage locker. Sometimes we are storing furniture to pass on to our children. Perhaps we should ask our children if they want it. They may prefer something very different, and would rather select their own new or used furniture when they are ready.

Storage lockers are a boon when we are in transition, or if, for some other reason, we need temporary storage for our furniture and other possessions. The key word, however, is temporary. I have several acquaintances who have been storing their extra possessions for years. They cannot even remember what is in the storage locker, nor can they face going back to deal with its contents. If you find yourself in such a situation, consider asking a friend, or someone else who is objective about the items, to empty the storage locker. Tell them to sell the contents, or give them to charity. You could offer to share the proceeds, or pay them a fee to perform this helpful service.

Think of the expense of keeping a locker for years. The rent can range from a minimum of $30, to $75 or more per month. This amounts to $360 to $900 per year. It may not be much on a monthly basis, but when it stretches into several years, it is a significant amount. Often the items stored are not worth the expense, and are no longer considered desirable when they are finally retrieved many years, and thousands of dollars, later. It's something for us to think about. If you have a storage locker, perform Exercise 4–2.

Exercise 4–2   Review your need for a storage locker

Consider what you have just read, and decide if the items in your storage locker should be retained, reduced, or cleared out. Can you remember what the locker contains? How much have you spent on storage so far? If the items have been in storage for years, plan to take some action to recycle them.

Once we dispose of our unused possessions, they quickly lose their hold on us. While it is often hard to part with them, within a few weeks or months, we usually can't remember what we gave away. Sometimes we'll retain fond memories of the part some of them once played in our lives. I know from experience that it isn't necessary to store the items in order to enjoy the memories. One woman, who found it impossible to part with some special clothes, had several photographs taken while wearing them. With the photographs as a memento, she was able to release the clothes.

Consider recycling those possessions that you are storing, or that are cluttering your space. It is easier to let something go when we know that someone else will enjoy it. We also have the satisfaction of knowing that we are making a contribution that helps reduce the use of our dwindling natural resources.

Reduce the clutter, reclaim your space

Clothes, clothes and more clothes — How does your clothes closet look? Is it filled with clothes you never wear? Perhaps they no longer fit you, or your lifestyle; you never liked them; they are worn out; they are out of style; or you are tired of wearing them. Usually there are certain garments that we favor and enjoy. The rest of them hang there, taking up precious space, adding to the clutter in our closet.

If you have not worn a garment in the past two years, it's unlikely that you ever will. Why not recycle those clothes? It is helpful to ask a friend whose taste you admire and whose opinion you respect to spend a few hours helping you decide which clothes should go. It may not be easy—we are attached to those clothes—nevertheless, the result is worth the effort. Your friend is objective, without emotional attachment to the clothes. Put on each garment, and follow the advice of your friend to let it go, or to keep it and begin wearing it again. You can do the same for your friend. I have a relative who does this for me. She also packs up the discarded clothes and takes them with her, so that I won't be tempted to return some to the closet. She sees that they are recycled, and find good homes.

You will be delighted at how much lighter and freer you will feel, and how much simpler your life will be with only the clothes you enjoy, and actually wear, in your closet. In a few days you will forget the clothes that are gone. You weren't wearing them anyway, were you?

If the shoe fits — Shoes are another item that we never seem to discard. They are worn out, not in style, or no longer suitable; yet we allow them to take up valuable closet space. After all, we might need that color again, or may decide to wear them some day. If you haven't had them on for a year or more, you will discover that they won't even feel comfortable when you try them on. Keep the shoes you wear, and let the rest go. You will never miss them, but you will value the empty space, and the relief of not having to deal with those unworn shoes. Begin to take some action by performing Exercise 4–3.

Exercise 4–3   Recycle your unworn clothes and shoes

Ask a friend or relative to help you decide which clothes and shoes you should keep, and which you should recycle. If you don't need this objective opinion, do it alone. Put on each garment, and follow the advice of your friend to let it go, or keep it and begin wearing it again. Keep only the shoes you wear in each season.

Everything but the kitchen sink — Take a look at the space under the kitchen sink. We have no emotional attachment to almost empty containers of cleaning supplies that are never used. Finish using them, or clear them out, and enjoy the pleasure of reclaiming this space.

Look in the kitchen cupboards and drawers. Recycle the excess plastic containers, and plastic bags. Six are probably all that you require for storing leftover food. Sell or give away all of your unused, duplicate, and unnecessary pots, dishes, utensils and stainless steel cutlery.

Check the space under the bathroom sink, in the medicine cabinet, and in the bathroom cupboards and drawers. They will yield outdated medicines, never used toiletries, almost empty bottles of old cosmetics, and unused samples. Feel the relief of using, recycling, or tossing out these items.

Basement, attic and garage — Consider eliminating your stored and unused furniture, appliances, tools, books, ornaments, as well as outgrown toys, and children's furniture or clothing. You could hold a garage sale, run a classified ad, give them to a friend, or donate them to one of the charities whose members may pick up the items.

A workshop participant suggested that we sell the items we are not attached to; then give the things we value most to friends or charity. Somehow this is easier, she explained. If we value the possession, it is hard to sell it for a lot less than it is worth. On the other hand, it will give us a sense of satisfaction to give it away. I did this myself, and I agree.

The paper chase — How the paper accumulates. You may have bank statements and canceled checks dating back ten, twenty or thirty years. You will gain a genuine sense of accomplishment from sorting and discarding most of those records. Keep your records for only seven years. Those that pertain to real estate, investments, or other important business, should be retained until you no longer own the property; and for three years after you file your income tax return.

Clear out recipes you have clipped and collected, but have never liked or tried. When I review them again, I realize that I'll never use them. Spend time reading your old greeting cards and letters, then part with those that don't have special meaning for you. Greeting cards can be recycled to create gift tags, or donated to some children for their enjoyment.

When the current magazine arrives, pass on the previous issue to a person or organization that will appreciate it. Tear out articles you want to read or keep. Stop your subscription to newspapers and magazines that you don't have time to read. Those unread periodicals clutter your space, and can seem to reproach you with their presence.

Feel freer without the clutter

How much lighter and freer we feel after clearing out the possessions we have been storing without using. It reduces the clutter and complexity in our space, and the burden in our lives. Begin with the things that carry no emotional attachment: under the sinks, the medicine cabinet, old financial records and recipes, and move on from there. Once you begin, the sense of relief can motivate you to continue until you have uncluttered your home.

To help keep your space uncluttered and simple, consider owning only a few well-chosen utensils and tools. Try to keep only the belongings you need, enjoy using, that give you pleasure, or that have a great deal of meaning for YOU. Some of us feel burdened by possessions we believe we must keep because they have been in the family for years. The person who enjoyed them is no longer here. If you don't want them, ask if there are other relatives who do. If no one else wants them, do you have to feel guilty about selling them, or giving them away? Will someone else take up the burden when you are no longer here? Remember, they could be used and appreciated by someone else. So seriously consider releasing them — and your guilt.

Learn to say, "No thank you"

Don't buy something just because it is a bargain. I carefully consider acquiring another possession, whether it is offered for free, it is a bargain, or it costs the retail price. I don't want to clutter my space and my life with unwanted or unneeded belongings. Think what you will do with the item, where you will put it, and how you will eventually dispose of it, before adding another possession to your care. You will have to work at keeping your life simple and uncluttered, but you can learn to say, "No thank you," to that extra possession you are offered free, or tempted to buy.

Pause now to perform Exercise 4–4 and consider some changes that would simplify your living space.

Exercise 4–4 How could you simplify your space?

How could you simplify your living space? Would you like to create a quiet, tranquil area for yourself? What else would you like to do to simplify your home? Make a note of the changes that come to mind, and plan to act on them.

The unseen energy of your home

Are you aware of the atmosphere, or energy, of your home? This is an often unrecognized, but very important element. A warm, nurturing energy, or a feeling of peace and harmony, can make even a lightly furnished room feel warm and comfortable. On the other hand, the most elaborately furnished home, if devoid of nurturing energy, will feel cold, sterile, and even empty. The inner and unseen richness, as with our own lives, is an important aspect.

Your home absorbs your energy, reflecting back to you, and all who enter, the quality of your inner life, and the warmth of the relationships you enjoy there. Most of us respond to the energy of our surroundings without conscious awareness; we simply know that a room is cozy, and that we feel nurtured, or at peace there. Indeed, as Dryden said, "Home is the sacred refuge of our life."

Summary

There is a sense of tranquillity in an uncluttered room that is furnished simply, and enhanced with some well-chosen accessories. Decide what makes you feel comfortable at home. Ask yourself if your house is larger than you require. The larger your house, and the more numerous your possessions, the higher your expenses, and the greater the burden in your life.

Think about clearing out your unused possessions, unworn clothes, and the accumulated paperwork of years. Commit to reducing this clutter and reclaiming your space. Empty your storage locker when the items do not warrant the expense, and have just been in storage for years. Recycle extra possessions by selling them or giving them away.

Remember, you can learn to say, "No thank you" to that extra possession you are offered for free, or are tempted to buy.

CREATING SIMPLICITY IN YOUR LIVING SPACE

GOALS

Short Term: 1 – 3 months

Goal: Clear out the clutter in the kitchen and bathroom

> **Action:** a) Eliminate unused items under the sinks
>
> b) Recycle extra items in the cabinets and drawers

Goal: Dispose of outdated and unnecessary paper

> **Action:** a) Throw out bank statements and canceled checks over seven years old
>
> b) Throw away clipped recipes that I never use
>
> c) Keep only current periodicals. Tear out articles I want to keep
>
> d) Discard old cards and letters. Retain only those I still value
>
> e) Recycle greeting cards
>
> f) Organize paperwork that remains

Goal: Clean out storage locker

> **Action:** a) Decide if the items will be used again
>
> b) Make sure the stored items are worth the expense of storage
>
> c) Ask for help, if necessary

Intermediate: 3 – 6 months

Goal: Clear out unused and unwanted clothing, shoes, accessories

> **Action:** a) Ask a friend or relative to help make decisions, if necessary
>
> b) Recycle the clothing by selling or giving it to charity

Goal: Dispose of other duplicate, unused and unneeded items

      Action: a) Decide which tools, books, ornaments, kitchenware, appliances, furniture, and outgrown children's items can go

                    b) Recycle by selling or giving them away

Long Term: 6 months – 1 year

Goal: Attain and maintain an uncluttered living space

Goal: Decide what I want to change in my home, and do it

      Action: a)_____

                    b)_____

CHAPTER 5

TAKING CONTROL OF YOUR FINANCES

Telling your money where to go, instead of wondering where it went

—*C. E. Hoover*

Taking control of our finances is an integral part of a balanced, simple lifestyle. When we simplify our lives, it is easier to take control of our finances; as we take control of our finances, it helps us to simplify our lives.

When we take command of our income we can spend wisely, save on a regular basis, pay our debts, and stay out of debt. By making a spending plan, or budget, we can see how much money we have at our disposal, the amounts we have designated for our fixed and changing expenses, and the amount we are saving for future goals.

Keeping track of expenses

Before we create our spending plan, we must know how we have been using our income. Acquire this information by keeping track of all your expenses for an entire month. It may sound like a daunting task, or just too much trouble, but without this data, you won't know where to begin. Start now by completing Exercise 5–1.

Exercise 5–1   Keep a record of your expenses

Carry a small notebook for an entire month, and record all of your expenditures. Under each day's date indicate the item, the amount spent, and whether you paid by cash, debit card, check, or credit card. Put down everything—your morning coffee and muffin, your lunch, your afternoon candy bar or piece of fruit, the gasoline for your car, your haircut, the total for each trip to the supermarket. Retain your grocery receipts to give you a record of each item purchased, and the amount spent. Be sure to do this every day for a month.

You will find this information valuable, even if you don't create a budget. If you have never kept track of how much you spend, you may be surprised at how quickly your expenses add up. This knowledge alone could encourage you to change your spending habits. With your record of a month's expenses, you will be ready to create your budget. We will discuss that later in this chapter, but first, let's consider various ways to alter your spending habits and simplify your life.

Those seemingly small expenditures

Think of a sales person who takes the cost of an expensive item, and breaks it down into small daily payments. "If you can afford $1.85 a day for your morning coffee," they may tell us, "then you can afford this $1,000.00 sofa; it will cost only $1.67 per day." Faced with such logic, we may agree. But let's take the opposite approach and consider some of our seemingly small expenses.

Suppose we eat lunch in a restaurant five days a week, spending approximately $6.00 per day. It may surprise you to discover that in one year—over a period of fifty weeks—we will spend $1,500.00. That sizable sum might profitably be spent in some other way: We could apply it towards paying a debt, save for something specific, add it to our savings account, or use it for something more important than eating lunch in a restaurant every day. We could choose to carry our lunch four days a week, or more, limiting the number of times we eat in a restaurant. This will not only reduce our expenses, but will convert a daily habit into a special occasion. One workshop participant declared that he had given up eating lunch in a restaurant to save for next year's trip to London.

Many of us spend from $4.00 to $6.00 to purchase our luncheon sandwich. If we buy food to prepare a lunch during our regular grocery shopping trips, it won't take more than five minutes to make and pack a lunch each day. We can do it in the morning, or the night before, storing it in the refrigerator overnight. By packing a lunch, we will effectively earn one hour's minimum wage for five minute's work. When we become aware of how these seemingly small expenditures add up, we can decide if we are using our income to best advantage.

We could save thousands of dollars in one year, by following this simple procedure for certain foods, and a number of our personal and entertainment expenses. How much do we spend on packaged snacks, candy, cookies, soft drinks, etc.? The list could be lengthy, and the dollar amounts quite high, if we make these items a routine part of our diet. If we bought them as an occasional treat, both our bank account and our health would benefit, and we would have something special to anticipate. Note the suggestions for saving at the supermarket in Table 5–A.

Table 5–A

SAVING AT THE SUPERMARKET
1. Create a master list of items you normally buy. Make copies of the list.
2. Check the items you need on a copy of the list. Limit purchases to items checked.
3. Review newspaper ads, coupons and in-store specials. Use only for items you normally purchase, or plan to buy when the price is reduced.
4. Buy in bulk when it is practical. Take into account storage required, and how long it will take you to use the item.
5. Buy nonperishable foods from the bulk food bins. These include: rice, pasta, cereal, nuts, beans, herbs, spices, teas, etc. This is more economical and cuts down on packaging materials required. Although herbs and spices look expensive by the pound, you can spend fifty cents or less for the small amount you require. By purchasing smaller quantities, you will have fresher herbs and spices in your cupboard.
6. Ignore tempting food displays, which encourage impulse shopping.
7. Compare prices of different brands when buying canned and packaged foods. Notice the unit price when comparing brands and quantities, but don't buy more than you can use.
8. Buy only enough fresh produce to last a week. This prevents spoilage and waste. Choose the best, and store in plastic bags in your refrigerator.
9. Buy certain fresh fruits and vegetables when they are in season, when prices are lowest. Compare the cost of asparagus in the spring, in contrast to other times of the year.

What are your annual expenses for special foods, as well as your personal and entertainment costs? Complete Exercise 5–2 to determine this amount.

> **Exercise 5–2   Determine your annual expenses for special items.**
>
> Maintain a list of your expenditures for candy, cookies, snacks and soft drinks for one full month. Do the same for your entertainment and personal expenses. Multiply by twelve to determine your annual expense. Decide to eliminate some of these items if you feel it is warranted, or desirable.

Debt, who needs it?

Would you like to earn up to 18% interest on your money? You can, by paying the balance due on your credit cards as quickly as possible. By lowering these balances, and eventually paying them in full, you will reduce and then eliminate the interest you pay for these loans. It's the same as earning that amount of interest on your money. These figures from "Money Talk" by Deborah Rankin demonstrate the extent of interest expense. "Assume you have an outstanding balance of $2,000 on a credit card charging 19.8% interest, and that you make only the minimum payment each month. It will take almost 42 years, and cost $9,637 to eradicate that debt. Every $20 item charged will have actually cost over $96. Paying $10 more each month will cost $5,382, and take 11-1/2 years to eliminate the debt."

You could make it a priority to pay your credit card debts in full, and choose to stop making further credit purchases. When your debts are paid, limit yourself to one credit card. This is all you require, if you only charge a purchase when you will have sufficient funds to pay the entire balance on the first month's due date. It gives you the benefit and convenience of borrowing money without interest for one billing cycle.

I prefer to pay cash, or use my debit card. I deduct the amount promptly from my checking account balance, as I do when writing a check, or withdrawing cash from the automatic teller machine (ATM).

It is mainly because we are unconscious of how we are spending our income, that we find ourselves unable to save, and carrying debts in various amounts. Living without debt, with adequate savings, is freedom. Think about paying off your debts as stated in Exercise 5–3.

Exercise 5–3   Commit to paying off your debts

Make the commitment to pay off your current debts as quickly as possible, and to live without creating further debt.   If you resist this, ask yourself why, and think about the consequences.

Consider the suggestions in Table 5–B to help you simplify and save.

Table 5–B

HOW TO SIMPLIFY AND SAVE

1. Purchase items that are functional, durable and attractive, and not necessarily inexpensive. Furniture, appliances, and tools can last for years, when well made, and treated with care.

2. Sometimes used items are better than new, and may be purchased at a fraction of the cost. Older furniture and appliances are often made with superior material and workmanship, and may be refinished.

3. Purchase clothes that are attractive as well as practical. With proper care, you will enjoy them for years.

4. With proper maintenance you can keep your machinery looking good and running well for years.

5. Repair and mend clothes, furniture, and appliances when possible.

6. Items that are seldom used, and are needed just for a day or specific purpose, may be rented, borrowed, or purchased jointly with other people you know. Rental companies carry tools, furniture, dishes, and more.

7. Don't buy something just because it is a bargain. Acquire only possessions that you need and like.

The difference between necessities and desires

We often hear people with sizable incomes complain that they don't make enough to purchase everything they desire. Apart from the very wealthy, however, who does? It isn't wise to go indiscriminately into debt, in order to satisfy every passing whim. When we do, we are mortgaging our lives.

Think about simplifying your life, and letting your values determine your priorities. Buy things for their usefulness, not as a status symbol. Our requirements for shelter, clothing, food and transportation might resemble the following column on the left, but when charged with emotion, move toward the column on the right.

Simple Necessities	Charged with Emotion
Comfortable home	Large prestigious house
Clothing that meets our needs	Expensive designer clothes
Nutritious Food	Meals in expensive restaurants
Reliable Transportation	Luxury automobile(s)

Learn to differentiate between *necessities* and *desires*, and simplify your life by delaying gratification of your desires.

Simple Necessities	Desires
A comfortable home	A new carpet
Clothing that meets our needs	New running shoes
Nutritious food	A new stereo
Reliable transportation	A vacation trip

Practice delaying gratification

As I mentioned in Chapter 3, when you have the impulse to buy something new, whether a stereo, a magazine subscription, another coat, or anything else, ask yourself if you really need it. Chances are the answer will be NO. Then forego making that purchase. I have effectively used this system to control my expenses since graduating from school and assuming responsibility for my own finances. If your answer is YES, try delaying gratification for a week, a month, or longer. In the interim, you could change your mind. Sometimes during this period, the item will come to you in an unexpected way: A friend may give it to you, you may find one somewhere for next to nothing without even looking for it, or something else may occur. If this happens, acknowledge it to yourself and express appreciation. By delaying gratification you will end impulse shopping, eliminate unnecessary debt, save money and reduce the clutter in your space.

You may decide after a lapse of time that you still desire the item, and want to make the purchase. If after allowing for necessities you don't have sufficient funds to cover the expense, you could begin to save for it. As you save, your anticipation will enhance your appreciation and enjoyment of the item. It's similar to the extra pleasure we derive from planning, and looking forward to a vacation trip or special event. One participant in my workshop enthusiastically reported that she and her husband had saved for six years in order to pay cash to remodel their kitchen. "We have never stopped appreciating that new kitchen," she declared.

Another class member remarked that she derived so much pleasure from researching, and planning to buy something new, that it was actually a bit of a letdown after she bought it. "I began to wonder if I should just do the research and then forget about making the purchase," she said with a laugh. That's not a bad idea, is it? Perhaps we can get the same result by changing our mind about making a purchase, after we have been saving for it for several weeks or months. Regardless of the outcome, whether we make the purchase or not, we won't find ourselves carrying the burden of debt, and paying up to 18% interest or more for the privilege.

When we decide to save for a particular goal, and know what the item will cost, we can determine how much we can save each month to reach our goal. Then we can calculate how long we must save to make the purchase. If the item has a deadline, such as tickets for an event or a vacation trip, we can figure out how much we must put aside each month to meet the deadline. We will probably have current goals, short-term goals, and long-term goals, depending on the cost of the items. We may want to save for a child's college education, or the down payment on a home, as examples of long-term goals. Some possible current and short-term goals could be a concert ticket, a camera, a washing machine, or a vacation trip. We could also save toward large semi-annual or annual expenses, such as real estate taxes, insurance premiums, or Christmas gifts. We might also save in order to pay off a debt as quickly as possible.

By preparing a schedule of our savings goals, we will know how much we must save each month to achieve them.. Create a schedule by completing Exercise 5–4.

Exercise 5–4   Your savings goals

Create and maintain a schedule of your savings goals. After you know the cost of an item, determine how much you can save each month, and the number of months it will take to reach your goals. When you have long-term goals, determine how much you can save each month, with or without a time frame. You could list your goals under these headings:

Goal   Estimated Cost   Monthly Savings   Time Required

Many of us go into burdensome debt because we believe that we should have absolutely everything we desire. When I was a child in Scotland, my parents taught me to save for something special, and how I valued the item when I bought it. To this day, I will do without, or delay gratification, rather than go into debt. We can teach our children the value of money, and how to question the wisdom of making a frivolous purchase. If we encourage them to save for something special, they will learn to appreciate, and value their possessions. They will also experience the added pleasure that comes from delayed gratification. These lessons and values will stand them in good stead for the remainder of their lives.

Let your values determine your priorities

As you simplify your life, you can let your values determine your priorities. Some of us value education, or travel. When these intangibles are more important than many material possessions, we may decide to do without, to postpone a purchase, or to acquire something second-hand. The money saved will be available for education or travel. Others may value having their own home, a large collection of books, or beautiful furnishings. Whatever you value can be your priority, and where you will spend your money, after making provision for necessities.

If you would like to have more free time, you could choose to simplify, and live at a lower economic level, so that you can reduce the number of your working hours. Others may elect to live below their current income, and invest the extra funds, give to worthwhile causes, or use it in other ways that they choose. As we simplify, our values may change, and we can establish new priorities. Complete Exercise 5–5 to determine your current priorities, and decide where you want to focus on spending your extra funds.

You can take more control of your finances by changing your attitude toward possessions, differentiating between necessities and desires, eliminating debt, delaying gratification, becoming aware of the consequences of your choices, and letting your values determine your priorities.

Creating your budget

You will be ready to create your first month's budget after you have kept track of your expenses for an entire month, completed the exercises throughout this chapter, and considered the various ideas for simplifying and saving.

Make a master, and several copies, of the budget pages in the appendix at the end of the book, or modify them to meet your needs. You may also duplicate the worksheets, or change them to meet your specific expenses. As one workshop participant facetiously pointed out to me, "You forgot a column for Starbucks."

Alternatively, you could purchase a budget booklet at an office supply store. These cost a few dollars and provide forms for several months. Or you may prefer to use one of the budget software programs for your computer.

"General guidelines for preparing your budget," and detailed "Instructions for preparing your budget" precede the budget forms in the appendix. You may find it helpful to read these pages no matter which format you use for your budget, or even if you don't prepare a budget. They will give you an overall picture of how to manage your income. When you are ready, create your first month's budget by completing Exercise 5–6.

Exercise 5–6   Prepare your first month's budget

Prepare your first month's budget, after maintaining an accurate record of your expenditures for one month, and completing the rest of the exercises in this chapter. Budget forms and worksheets, preceded by step-by-step instructions, are in the appendix at the end of the book. If you prefer, you may purchase a budget booklet or a software program for your computer.

Managing your money with minimum structure

You can also develop a less structured way of managing your income, after you have prepared and followed your budget for several months or years. This is possible when you have a true sense of your income and expenses, have simplified your life, are saving regularly, and are living debt free.

For example, you could decide to save a certain percentage of your income every month, and consciously live on what remains. After deducting the amount you have chosen to save, you put aside the amount necessary for your *fixed expenses*, and other necessities such as food and transportation. Then you can determine whether you have enough for extras such as a movie, new clothes, or dining out. This is basically how I manage my money, and it works something like this. I remembered one day that I had intended to buy some produce before returning home, and discovered that my wallet contained only $8.00. As I shopped, I focused on the most important items, and kept a running total in my head—carrots, $1.00; broccoli, $1.50, etc. When my cumulative total was approximately $0.50 short of $8.00, I stopped and checked out the items. I had $0.23 left, everything I needed, but nothing left for extras. You get the idea. By setting aside the amount needed for essentials, and being conscious of how much you are spending, you can judge whether you have enough for extras.

Remember, to successfully use this method, you must be fully aware of your expenses, be debt free, be saving regularly, and be disciplined about your desires. You may also use this example as a springboard for creating your own variation of this plan.

The more you increase your awareness, change your attitude toward possessions, and simplify and save, the easier it becomes to take control of your finances, and enjoy the freedom, peace of mind and other opportunities this creates.

Summary

As you take more control of your finances, you increase the opportunity to simplify your life. The more you simplify your life, and eliminate unnecessary expenses, the easier it becomes to take control of your finances.

You can begin by changing your attitude toward possessions, and learning to differentiate between necessities and desires. You can let your values determine your priorities, and practice delaying gratification to eliminate debt. You may use your income to best advantage by asking yourself if you really need it, buying things for their usefulness and not as a status symbol, and becoming aware of your seemingly small expenditures.

When you save on a regular basis, and eliminate debt, you will enjoy the freedom and opportunity this creates. The rewards will be reflected in every area of your life.

TAKING CONTROL OF YOUR FINANCES

GOALS

Short Term: 1 – 3 months

Goal: Become conscious of my spending habits

    Action: a) Carry a small notebook, and keep track of every expenditure for one month. Record the date, the item, amount spent, and how paid

Goal: Determine my total n*et income* for one month

Goal: Create a record of my current *fixed expenses* for one month

Goal: Compile a record of my *changing expenses* for one month

Goal: Based on my actual monthly expenses (derived from my notebook), decide what changes to make in my spending habits

    Action: a) Determine if my money is being spent to best advantage

                      b) Decide where I could cut back and do without

Intermediate: 3 – 6 months

Goal: Determine my priorities, based on my values

    Action: a) Decide what is important to me: travel, my own home, more free time, etc

                      b) Choose where to cut back on expenses, taking into account suggestions for saving

                      c) Decide whether to concentrate on eliminating debts

Goal: Take charge of how I spend my income

    Action: a) Create a goals schedule for things I desire

                      b) Prepare a simple budget for one month

                      c) Strive to live within my budget for one month

Goal: Start a regular savings plan, or build on one I already have

    Action: a) Have separate funds for emergencies, specific goals, and a savings program

                  b) Decide how much I will save on a regular basis

Long Term: 6 months – 1 year

Goal: Be in control of my finances

    Action: a) Have a budget that works

                  b) Simplify my finances

                  c) Be saving on a regular basis

                  d) Be paying off debts previously acquired

                  e) No longer buy on credit

CHAPTER *6*

ENHANCING THE QUALITY OF YOUR TIME

You will never find time for anything. If you want time, you must make it.
—*Charles Buxton*

On a stroll through the park one day, I paused to watch a small girl riding a merry-go-round. Lying spread-eagled, face down on the floor, and clinging to the center, she called, "Faster, make it go faster," while her parents kept it spinning. It seemed to me a reflection of our madly whirling lives.

I thought of the merry-go-round we used to ride as children, and how we enjoyed the spin and the changing view. If someone increased the speed too much, however, everything became a blur. Like the child on this merry-go-round, we had to give all our attention just to hanging on. It really wasn't fun anymore, and how some of us longed to get off.

Lives crammed with constant action

Clearly, for so many of us, life has become a blur. We have to give too much attention just to hanging on. We have crammed our lives with constant action: We work long hours to meet our numerous obligations, pay our debts, and climb the ladder to success. We volunteer, belong to numerous organizations, attend various functions, meetings and events. We take care of our personal lives and our families, and shuttle our children to soccer, ballet, little league, and more. Whether employed full-time, or not, we rush headlong from one activity to another, compulsively filling every minute. We complain that we have no time, but often we have chosen to have no free time.

Caught in a stream of endless demands and activities, we seem to have lost the capacity to say No. Both men and women report feeling caught in this frenzied pace. Young parents, middle-aged people, a few who have recently left college, and some approaching, or living in retirement speak of their desire to slow this dizzying spin. We have not found the happiness we seek on the whirling merry-go-round, and many report feelings of emptiness and lack of fulfillment. We are ready to discover how less can be liberating in so many ways.

How are you spending your time? Do you know? If life is such a frantic blur that you don't know where the time goes, follow this variation of Richard Foster's suggestion, and perform Exercises 6–1 and 6–2 to help you see how to change that.

Exercise 6–1   Keep track of your various activities and obligations

Keep track of your various tasks, obligations, and pastimes for one week. How much time is involved, and how do you feel as you go through your activities every day? Use one word to describe your feelings or attitude. Did you find it satisfying, nourishing, frustrating, tiresome, inspiring, or boring, etc.? Create a worksheet and record your entries under these headings.

Activity	Time Spent	Feelings

Exercise 6.2   Categorize your activities

At the end of a week, group your activities under different headings. Include everything from doing the laundry and other chores, to your job, shopping, attending a concert, putting your child to bed, or reading a book.

(1) First there are things you alone must perform, by necessity or desire.

(2) Next, there are those that are necessary, but could be done by someone else.

(3) Then there are activities that are not essential.

Beside each listed activity include the word describing your feelings, and the amount of time involved.

Look at the activities under categories two and three above. If they are not giving you a sense of satisfaction or in some way nourishing your soul, try to eliminate, or delegate some. If you can afford it, you may have to pay for someone's service to create some time for yourself, or for a nurturing activity.

Evaluate the amount of time you spend in your work, and decide if it is consuming too much of your life. As you simplify your life and reduce your desires, you may be able to reduce your working hours. Next, give careful consideration to all new requests for your time, and be conscious of how you are choosing to spend it. You can learn to say No as well as Yes. Explain that you have another commitment, even if that commitment is to yourself and your need for some precious time alone. Unfortunately, this is often given the lowest priority. Yet, as Harriet Braiker, a stress researcher, notes, "Chronic overstimulation taxes the body's physiological system, and results in fatigue, debilitation and depletion of the immune system. Stress contributes to, or causes, just about any disease or illness."

The importance of solitude and silence

The effects of solitude and inner silence are just the opposite. Enjoy periods of silence by refraining from habitually turning on your television, radio, or stereo. When our senses are constantly overstimulated, they become numbed and dull. We require increasing levels of sound to catch and hold our attention, or to help us feel alive. It is the contrast—sound and silence, activity and rest, work and leisure, companionship and solitude—which enhances our pleasure in each of these experiences.

A workshop participant expressed astonishment after a week without listening to the radio in her car. "How I enjoyed the silence and the peace," she declared. "I realized for the first time how I had been unconsciously subjecting myself to endless chatter and music by habitually turning on the radio."

"My family worries because I have no radio in my car," another student remarked, "but I don't need one. If I want to be entertained, I play the small harmonica I carry in my car." She nurtures herself by creating music, and enhances her feeling of being alive.

I, too, live happily without a radio or tape deck in my car. I confess I like silence. When alone on a lengthy trip, I sometimes sing the Scottish songs from my childhood. It is nourishing and energizing. Try singing in your car. When alone in your car you can also practice developing your awareness. Become aware of the feel of the steering wheel in your hands, or of the seat against your back. Make use of your time spent sitting in traffic to enjoy some time alone, practicing inner silence, and experiencing moments of peace.

As with all contrast, when we become accustomed to spending part of our time in silence, less begins to feel like more.

"Since I started spending some time in meditation," a friend observed, "I find it more difficult to tolerate large crowds and ear-shattering sound levels. It makes me wonder if now I can't deal with the real world."

Is our culturally created hyper-activity the real world? The peace of a forest glade, the crash of ocean surf, the trill of the birds, the laughter of children at play, all are different sounds of the real world. They create peace, tranquillity, and joy. Our society values action and achievement, but with growing awareness, we will recognize the importance of spending part of each day in silence. "Meditation is a way of being," states Jon Kabat Zinn, "It is like weaving a parachute, day in and day out, so that when you need it, it will hold you. We should create some time every day just as a time for being." You will find it creates an inner calm that underlies most of your actions, and that it is easier to return to your own center after times of stress.

Take a few minutes now to "create some time for being." Perform Exercise 6–3 to deepen the inner silence you began to experience with Exercise 2–5.

Exercise 6–3   "Create some time for being"

Sit in a comfortable position with your back straight and feet flat on the floor. Close your eyes, or look at the floor. Exhale, then take a deep breath, inhaling all the way down into your abdomen. Now slowly let it out. Repeat three times. This will help to center you, and silence your mind. Continue to watch the rise and fall of your breath. When thoughts arise, have no interest in them; simply let them dissolve, and return your attention to the rise and fall of your breath. Now extend your awareness out five feet from your body. Breathe into that space. After a few more breaths, extend your awareness out to fill the room. Continue to breathe into that space while you sit in inner silence. After several minutes, when you feel ready, bring your awareness back to your body, and open or raise your eyes.

Reclaiming our boundaries

Many of us complain that our boundaries are being invaded; that we can be reached anywhere, anytime with our cellular telephones, pagers, and fax machines. We make the choices, however. We are not completely at the mercy of the growing number of machines that fill our lives. We decide whether to use the fax machine, or own the cellular telephone, then to carry it everywhere, and answer every call whether or not it is necessary for our profession. Our material possessions should enhance the quality of our lives; we don't have to allow them to contribute to our feelings of frenzy. Choose whether to own a television or not, and when to turn it on. Take responsibility for what you are subjecting yourself to.

Limit your use of some machines

Washing machines, dryers, dishwashers, food processors, and other modern appliances and gadgets are intended to free us from the drudgery of everyday life, but do they? Instead of giving us more time for leisure, recreation and creativity, we are spending a great amount of time with a growing number of increasingly complex machines. Think before you add another, and yet another, machine to your life. Consider using some that are manually operated, silent, less expensive, and easier to maintain and repair. The hand-wound can-opener is more convenient, silent and easy to use. The hand-pushed manual lawn mower is quieter, easier to maneuver, kinder to the grass, and more appropriate for a small urban lawn.

Use the clothesline instead of the dryer some of the time, and wash some of your special clothes by hand. Enjoy some quiet moments at the sink, while you squeeze the suds through your delicate clothes, and rinse them two or three times. Gently squeeze out the water by hand, and allow your garment to dry on a hanger over the tub, or out on the line. Your clothes will retain their body and color for a longer period of time.

Clothes from the washing machine can also be hung on the clothes line to dry. While you pin your laundry on the line, you'll enjoy the song of the birds, the warmth of the sun, the caress of the breeze, and the vision of grass, flowers and trees. You will also delight in the wonderful scent of fresh air on your clothes. If you don't have many dirty dishes, wash and dry them by hand. These simple tasks will give you another opportunity to spend time alone, develop your awareness, and experience inner peace.

"When boys and girls come out to play"

Our children, too, lead structured, busy lives so filled with planned activities that they have little opportunity, or even inclination, to play alone or with friends. Most of us have fond memories of childhood. I remember delightful hours of freedom in Scotland, after school, homework and piano practice. How we loved to play in the fields at the end of our street, where we built our dens (forts) from branches, and old scraps of metal and wood. We swung on the gates between the fields, climbed over walls, or picked and ate blackberries. Sometimes we dawdled at the river, watching the minnows swim past, sailing our paper boats, or paddling our feet in the water. As a family, we sometimes had picnics in the park, day excursions to the hills, and holidays by the sea. I had tea parties with my dolls, and learned to embroider from my friend's older sister, while we sat outside on a low stone wall. In the evenings we played Monopoly, Snakes & Ladders, and other board games. Mom or Dad read to us, until we learned the pleasure of reading by ourselves. I remember walking alone to my piano lessons. We were also taught that it was fun to save, and to watch our money grow in our piggy banks.

If we don't, or can't, give our children free, unstructured time for imaginative play in their formative years, when will they have it? Will they ever know how to live less structured lives, if their early upbringing teaches them that compulsive busyness is the norm?

Help your children to enjoy quiet moments. They live naturally in the present, with a lively curiosity and interest in what lies before them. Give them time just to "be," and to express themselves in imaginative play. Show them the value and pleasure in quiet, creative activity. Introduce them to gentle, uplifting books. I still find pleasure in reading *Heidi, The Secret Garden*, and *Anne of Green Gables* to a child. When parents withstand the opposition, and turn off the television for a month or more, they find that after a week or two of dissent, their children are calmer and better behaved. Their ability to concentrate improves, and so does their school work. They soon learn how to play and entertain themselves, either alone or with siblings; and you can teach them, or they will discover, the pleasure of reading.

Some workshop participants express their desire to teach their children the values and pleasures of simpler living. You can give the gift of simplicity to yourself, and pass it on to your children. Try giving them some quality attention, and an introduction to the joys of simple pleasures. In the process, you will enrich their lives and yours.

Eliminate the extra stuff

Our lives are filled with extra stuff: extra activities, extra possessions, extra clutter in our heads. When we get to the core, or the heart of things, our activities are balanced and enrich our lives, as well as adding to the quality of life of those around us. Our possessions reflect our requirements for practical and aesthetic reasons, with a minimum of excess baggage. Our heads are clear, and we are present in the moment. We experience heightened awareness, and a sense of inner connection and of peace.

Hyacinths for your soul

"If nothing remains in your storehouse but two loaves of bread, you should sell one loaf, and with the proceeds, buy some hyacinths for your soul." This rather well-known adage, attributed to both the ancient Persians and Chinese, indicates the importance of nourishing both body and soul. Today, with our lives overcrowded with obligations, activities, and the accumulation of endless possessions, we are sorely in need of some hyacinths for the soul. You can choose to "sell one loaf"—to begin to simplify your life—and with the time and space you create, to cultivate and grow some hyacinths for your soul.

Take time to think about what is important to you, by answering the questions posed in Exercise 6–4.

Exercise 6–4   What is important to you?

- Flash forward to the end of your life, and ask yourself what you would like to have accomplished and experienced when you look back. What kind of person would you like to have become? — Are you doing things now that will contribute to that end? Are you practicing the qualities that will lead you there?

- If you had only six months to live, how would you spend it? — What is preventing you from doing some of these things now, or planning to do them within the next year? If you say you would spend the time with your family, it is important to start spending more quality time with them now. If you say you would spend some of that time in travel, start saving regularly, and planning for a trip a year from now.

- What do you love to do that you don't have time for? — Why not create some time and start to do it soon?

Write down your answers to the questions in Exercise 6–4, and look at them from time to time. Change your responses when and if your priorities change. Use your answers to motivate yourself to take action, and to cultivate some hyacinths for your soul.

Enhance the quality of your time

To simplify your life, enhance the quality of your time, and cultivate some hyacinths for your soul:

- Turn off the television at least one day and evening per week. It may be too drastic to suggest that you give it up entirely, but you will discover that your life without the television is calmer and more authentic. Without television, you can live the life you choose, with more time for yourself, your family and friends, and the pursuit of activities and projects you find enjoyable and worthwhile. The often exaggerated version of life we participate in vicariously through the television, does not leave us energized, or enhance our feeling of being alive.

- Spend some time in your garden, in a park, in the mountains, or at the beach. Practice silence and meditation to refresh your soul. Just sit quietly with a cup of tea, sipping and savoring the steaming brew. Listen to the rain pattering on the leaves, on your window, or on the roof. Watch and listen to the wind rustle through the trees. Observe the changing patterns of the clouds.

- Enjoy moments of creativity: Bake and cook from scratch from time to time. Enjoy the sensory satisfaction of kneading bread dough by hand, and the aroma of freshly baked bread. Sew a garment for yourself or your children, or create some fancy needlework. Arrange some flowers to lift your spirits and beautify your home. Plant and tend a garden. If you don't have your own plot of ground, plant flowers or vegetables in pots for your patio or porch, rent some space in a community garden, or offer to help your friends tend their piece of land. Learn to paint or wallpaper, try simple carpentry, or plumbing and electrical repair. What other crafts or hobbies have you wanted to pursue? Make a note of them, and begin to incorporate them into your life.

- Renew your sense of connection by writing letters to friends and relatives you rarely see. We all enjoy the sense of anticipation and pleasure when we receive a letter in the mail. Have evenings with family and friends for conversation, games and laughter. Develop and maintain some close friendships; how they add to the richness of life. I learned when I was young, that friendship, like a garden, has to be cultivated and nourished to bloom and grow. Both wither and die through neglect. If you have some old and valued friendships that have languished, take some time to renew and revitalize these relationships.

- Find time for inspiration by reading uplifting books, listening to classical music, enjoying beauty in all its forms in art or nature.

- Experience pleasure and refreshment in some of your favorite pastimes and pursuits. Take a moment to think of some you enjoy.

- Energize your body by walking, swimming, jogging, cycling, or in other forms of exercise.

- Try camping to bring you closer to the natural world and the great outdoors, and to allow you to experience "living with only the essential facts of life."

- Consider hosteling through Hosteling International as an inexpensive form of simple travel. You will meet other adventuresome people from around the world, and enjoy the camaraderie this form of travel promotes.

Incorporate what you value into your life

What do you value? In what small ways can you begin to incorporate these activities into your life? As Marsha Sinetar writes, "The point is to identify the things that light us from within." What "lights you from within"? Is it being in the natural world, reading uplifting books, painting, writing, spending time with your family? Take time to answer the questions in Exercise 6–5, and resolve to make some changes. Begin to incorporate the activities you value into your days.

Exercise 6–5   What do you want to incorporate into your life?

- How could you simplify your schedule? What changes could you make?

- What activities and pastimes would you like to incorporate into your life?

Make a note of your answers. Begin to take some action to make them part of your life.

Reflections on a simple life

Carey, a vice president and successful broker with a large investment firm in Seattle, has all of the accouterments of a successful life: a lovely family, a beautiful home, a six figure income, a luxurious car, and more. I enjoy talking to Carey. With all of these symbols of success, he still remembers with nostalgia his experience of living in utmost simplicity as a younger man.

"Some day I would like to return to a simpler lifestyle," he ruefully confesses. "I felt so alive and in touch with life then. Now, because of my position, I am part of what Voltaire called, 'the parade of wealth.' I must maintain all of the embellishments that go with this lifestyle. Still, the memory of that early experience is always with me, and I find refreshment, when I need it, by recalling how I felt at that simpler time. But when I retire—"

This is how Carey describes his early experience in simple living.

"I was selling real estate at that time. I had just left college, and was still single. I purchased an acre of land far out in the countryside, and had a clearing made in the woods. I bought a simple, single-wide mobile home, second-hand, and had it put out there in the clearing.

"I had no power that far from the city, of course, so I used a kerosene lamp for light, and a wood-burning stove for heat. I did a little bit of cooking on a two-burner camp stove. I had to pack my water in, using a plastic bag, and I carried it for a mile through a path I had cut in the woods. As I had no refrigeration, I ate canned food, and learned that whole-wheat bread kept longer than white.

"Although I lived so simply, I still went into the real estate office every day, and sold real estate in the area. I socialized with my friends, too. I can still remember so clearly, though, that wonderful feeling of release, when I left my car, and entered the peace and tranquillity of the woods for my mile walk home each night. I didn't even have to use a flashlight. I felt such a sense of happiness and contentment in my simple little home out there. I would open my can of beans, pour them into the pan, and put them onto the burner to heat. I found such satisfaction in eating those beans and my brown bread. How vivid everything was, and how connected I felt to the woods. It seemed as if I was part of them. I remember that six month period of simple living as one of the happiest times of my life."

Carey changed employers a few years ago, choosing one whose philosophy and management style gave him more personal satisfaction. He also creates time and opportunities to nurture his soul in ways that fit his current obligations and lifestyle: He is renovating a small historic hotel, coaches a little league team; spends time with his children; enjoys simple holidays with his family in a cabin on the Washington coast. They are also homeschooling two of their children so that they can experience some of the joys of a simpler life.

Like Carey, you, too, may feel you must continue in the current pattern of your life, at least for the present—you have a family to provide for, obligations to be met, and debts to be paid. Although you can't make all the changes you desire, you can start, right where you are, to make adjustments and alterations that create more balance in your life. You can enhance the quality of your time. Try not to postpone beneficial changes in your life. Don't put everything on hold until—. Only you can give yourself the gift of simplicity through the choices you make in each moment. It is easy to live with simplicity on a Greek island. It is possible to live with increasing simplicity wherever you are, when you make the decision, and the commitment, to simplify your life.

"We have time enough if we will use it aright." —Johann W. Goethe

Summary

We may rush from one activity to another, lamenting that we have no time. Often, however, it is we who have chosen to have no free time.

Notice how you are spending your time. Take note of your attitude toward your various activities and obligations. When possible, eliminate or delegate some, if they are not giving you satisfaction, or some other reward, Give careful consideration to all new requests for your time, and learn to say No as well as Yes.

Try limiting or controlling your use of some machines. Our material possessions should add to the quality of our lives, instead of contributing to its frustrations.

Enhance your life by creating time for solitude and practicing inner silence. Spend time in the natural world, whether it is your garden, a sunlit grove, or by the sea. Linger with family and friends over a cup of tea, or in playing a game. Find pleasure and inspiration in music, art and books. Exercise, and enjoy a favorite sport, hobby, or other form of recreation.

Give the gift of simplicity to your children by showing them how to enjoy quiet moments. Teach them the pleasure of reading, and encourage their imaginative play.

You can choose to incorporate the activities you value into your life, and to cultivate and grow some hyacinths for your soul.

ENHANCING THE QUALITY OF YOUR TIME

GOALS

Goal: Give careful consideration to all requests for my time

    Action: a) Learn to say No sometimes

                  b) Create some time for solitude and silence

Goal: Reclaim my boundaries

    Action: a) Choose when I will use the fax machine, cellular telephone, pager, etc.

Goal: Limit my use of some machines

    Action: a) Cut use of the power mower, clothes dryer, dishwasher, bread maker

                  b) Be selective in watching television

                  c) Refrain from turning on the television, radio, or stereo some of the time

Goal: Give my children the gift of simplicity

    Action: a) Give them some unstructured quiet time, and encourage their imaginative play

                  b) Teach them the pleasure of simple creative activity

                  c) Introduce them to gentle, inspiring books

                  d) Turn off the television for a month, and then limit, or eliminate, its use

                  e) Spend some quality time with them.

Goal: Cultivate some hyacinths for my soul

        Action: a) Spend some time in the natural world

                           b) Create some moments of peace and beauty

                           c) Enjoy time for creativity

                           d) Establish connection with friends and relatives

                           e) Find time for inspiration

                           f) Energize my body

Goal: Incorporate the activities I value into my life. These are:

        Action: a)_____

                           b)_____

                           c)_____

CHAPTER 7

FINDING SATISFACTION IN YOUR WORK

To love what you do and feel that it matters—how could anything be more fun?
—Katharine Graham

As you simplify your life and take control of your finances, you may experience greater freedom in your working life.

For a variety of reasons, many are working long hours. It may be to meet the increasing demands of the corporate world as a result of rapidly changing technology, mergers, and downsizing; or it may be in an effort to meet their numerous obligations. Some who have taken my class were working sixty hours a week, or more, while others had recently chosen to leave their stressful positions.

Need for rest and recuperation

You, like many others, may be experiencing burnout, fatigue, anxiety and other forms of stress from the excessive demands of your work. If you have these symptoms, make it a priority to alleviate them. If you have not completed the exercises in Chapter 6, turn to them again and clear some time for rest and recuperation. Create some inner peace by spending time in solitude and inner silence. Incorporate exercise and physical activity into your life to release excess adrenaline, loosen tight muscles, increase your energy, strength and endurance, and create some mood-enhancing endorphins. Make time for family and friends, and the enjoyment of simple pleasures to enhance your emotional well-being.

Simplify to increase your options

Some class members had taken a few months off to renew themselves and review their options, after leaving their stressful jobs. They felt liberated by the freedom they had enjoyed, and were ready to create something new. A few were considering part-time work. They will be able to take advantage of the job sharing opportunities offered by some companies, or part-time work that may or may not have the same prorated benefits as full-time positions. Other employers offer flex time to accommodate their employees' individual lifestyles.

Other class participants dreamed of creating a business of their own; or of returning to school, and improving their skills or learning new ones, in order to change their careers. All agreed that having adequate savings and freedom from debt had made such options possible. Whether currently employed, or in transition, all were ready to simplify in order to create a more balanced and rewarding life.

Some of us are choosing to move to a smaller community to escape the stress of city life. We enjoy the slower pace, and may have more opportunities to create a sense of belonging, and to contribute to the community. We may be able to take advantage of computer technology to work from home, perhaps linked to a corporation in another city. Or, we may find satisfaction in creating a business of our own.

I remember enjoying the simplicity and sense of community when I spent several months visiting relatives in the small Scottish town where I was born. I began the day with a walk down Main Street, stopping at the baker's, the newsagent's, the greengrocer's, and the co-op to buy groceries for the day. This half-hour stroll gave me a sense of camaraderie and belonging, as townsfolk and shopkeepers chatted and bantered together in the shops.

Take a moment to define your own ideal work and environment by answering the questions in Exercise 7–1.

Exercise 7–1   Create a profile of your ideal work and environment

Write a description of your ideal work and environment, incorporating the various aspects enumerated below.

1. Describe your work and tasks.

2. Are you being creative, or using particular skills or talents? What are they?

3. Do you work with things? Do you work with facts and figures? Do you have contact with the public?

4. Do you have a few specific responsibilities, or a lot of variety?

5. Is it challenging and busy, or somewhat relaxed?

6. Do you work alone, or with other people? How many people are in the company?

7. Do you work full-time, or part-time? How many hours? What hours?

8. Are you in business for yourself?

9. Are you in a profession?

10. Describe your surroundings.

11. Is the atmosphere formal or casual?

12. Are you in the city? Are you in a small town or rural community?

13. Add anything else that would complete your description of fulfilling work.

   Keep this profile and refer to it often. It could help you move toward something new.

Uncertainty can lead to something new

   Do you long to try something new? Do you have a talent you would like to express? Do you have an idea for a new product, or a worthwhile service, you would like to provide? Could you market it with success?

   It is easy to resist taking action on our ideas, or even to contemplate what we really want to do. I know; I have done it. Yet, when I finally overcame my resistance and took the first small step, I was thrilled with the enthusiastic response I received. It was then a matter of taking each succeeding step as it was required. I couldn't help thinking how close I came to missing these opportunities. Take time to complete Exercise 7–2. Ask yourself what you would do if you knew you could not fail, to help yourself uncover your aspirations.

> **Exercise 7–2   What would you do if you knew you could not fail?**
>
> What would you do if you knew you could not fail, and money were no object? Use your imagination. Let yourself go. Allow yourself to dream. Discuss it with your spouse or a friend, if you choose, to help to get your ideas flowing. Make a note of your answers. Now, consider the possibility of taking the first small step toward fulfillment of that ambition or goal.

It often takes courage to listen to inner promptings, and to act on the guidance we receive. It may not be necessary to take drastic action, however, but rather just the first small step, or perhaps a succeeding step, on our unfolding path. It's a moment-to-moment process, requiring courage, trust, and the willingness to live with a certain amount of uncertainty. When we focus our vision, then take the first small step, it can begin the unfolding process to the fulfillment of our dreams.

"If we want to do what we love, we must dare to try something new," Marsha Sinetar writes. The risk, however, should be well calculated. "We must feel strong enough to deal with our separation from the work, the company, and the lifestyle which has defined us, and given us a sense of security in the past," she cautions. If we are willing and able to work through the transition, however, the rewards could more than compensate for our efforts.

Volunteering

You may be able to satisfy some of your desires in volunteer work, if you can fit it into your schedule without undue stress. In addition to the intrinsic reward of helping others, you may have the opportunity to use some of your natural talents and abilities. You may learn new skills, meet different people, and make contacts that could help you in the future.

I was happy using my planning and organizational skills in one volunteer project. In another instance, I fould an outlet for my interest in good nutrition by working a few hours a week in a new section of the Employee Health Department of a large hospital.

Summary

As you cultivate the habit of living in the moment, bringing your full awareness to the task before you, you can improve your efficiency, increase your energy and enthusiasm, and find more satisfaction in your work.

As you simplify your life, reducing the clutter in your space, time, and mind, you can create the space for something new. When you take control of your finances, deliberately save, eliminate debt and strive to live within your means, you will know the sense of freedom this promotes. You may choose to review your options, take a calculated risk, and change the direction of your work and your life.

You may have a talent or skill you long to express, an idea you want to develop, or a service you want to provide. If you can live with a certain amount of uncertainty, trust the guidance you receive, and take the first, and each succeeding step, you may actualize your vision and realize your goal.

FINDING SATISFACTION IN YOUR WORK

GOALS

Goal: Find more satisfaction in my work

    Action: a) Bring full awareness to the task before me

                  b) Be aware of the needs and opportunities of each moment

                  c) Increasingly act on my own initiative

                  d) Increase my enthusiasm

                  e) Improve my skills and learn new ones

                  f) Further my education in various ways

Goal: Have time for rest and recuperation

    Action: a) Spend some time in solitude and inner silence

                  b) Maintain a regular exercise program

                  c) Spend time with family and friends

                  d) Have fun and enjoy some simple pleasures

Goal: Create the opportunity to use my talents and abilities

    Action: a) Look for ways to use them in my work

                  b) Employ them in volunteer work or a hobby

                  a) Overcome my resistance to trying something new

Goal: Experience meaningful involvement in my community

    Action: a) Volunteer in a satisfying capacity

                  b) Seek ways to experience connection and belonging

                  c) Consider becoming part of a small group, or community

CHAPTER **8**

PROMOTING HEALTH

Let your food be your medicine

—Hippocrates

When we embrace a simpler lifestyle, sooner or later we are drawn to lighter, more natural food. We may be motivated by the desire to simplify our diet, or to improve our health and sense of well-being; we may have a growing compassion for all life, and increasing concern for the earth's ecology. In this chapter we'll explore the first two reasons, turning to the others in Chapter 9.

Link between health and a vegetarian diet

Research from around the world confirms that a low-fat, high-fiber diet, focusing on fruits, vegetables, whole grains and legumes, improves our health and retards the aging process.

Seventh Day Adventists, who regularly follow this diet and avoid smoking, caffeine and alcohol, live approximately eight years longer than the general population. In addition, they suffer from few of the diseases associated with lifestyle such as osteoporosis, heart disease, cataracts, diabetes, and breast, prostate and colon cancer.

In 1995, the Alliance for Aging Research, after forty years' research, confirmed that a plant-based diet, with additional nutritional supplements, helped protect against the above-mentioned diseases, which we usually associate with aging. Books supporting the value of a low fat, vegan diet include Dr. Neal D. Barnard's, *Foods That Fight Pain,* John Robbins' *Diet for a New America*, and *Dr. Dean Ornish's Program for Reversing Heart Disease.*

Recent research shows that by the time children are nine years old, their blood vessels already contain fatty deposits. This plaque continues to build with the passing years. A study by Dr. Dean Ornish reveals that with a low-fat, vegan diet, regular exercise, and meditation, we can reverse this buildup in our blood vessels. After approximately three weeks on his program, heart disease patients begin to experience less pain and have more energy. Mutual of Omaha and several other insurance companies are so impressed with these findings that they will pay bypass surgery candidates if they will follow Dr. Ornish's program instead of having surgery.

You'll find the basis for some of the preceding findings in the sections on Fat and Fiber which follow.

Fat and cholesterol

We require a certain amount of fat to provide the essential fatty acids required for different bodily functions. Fats are mostly triglycerides, made up of three fatty acids attached to a sugar molecule (glycerol). Fatty acids are either saturated, monounsaturated, or polyunsaturated, depending on the number of hydrogen atoms on a chain of carbon atoms. Saturated fatty acids have the maximum number of hydrogen atoms. Mono-unsaturated fatty acids are missing one pair of hydrogen atoms. Polyunsaturated fatty acids are missing two, or more, pairs of hydrogen atoms. Thus, when polyunsaturated oils are hydrogenated, extra hydrogen atoms are added to the chain, making them saturated fats.

Research shows that the body benefits most from the monounsaturated oils such as olive, canola and peanut, followed by the polyunsaturated oils such as safflower, sunflower, and corn. Saturated fats from animal products, as well as palm oil, coconut oil and cocoa butter, should be almost eliminated. For better health, total fat consumption, no matter what the type, should be limited. The Food and Drug Administration recommends 30% of calories from fat, while some sources such as Dr. Ornish, recommend only 10%.

Cholesterol, a form of fat (or lipid) called a sterol, is not a triglyceride. This waxy, fat-like material is essential to life, and used to build cell membranes, protect nerve sheaths, and to produce vitamins and hormones. The liver makes the cholesterol our body requires. Cholesterol is not water soluble and travels through the bloodstream paired with proteins, in a combination called a lipoprotein (lipid plus protein). Lipoproteins can have a high density of protein (HDL), or more fat and a low density of protein (LDL). LDL, commonly referred to as the bad cholesterol carrier, transports most of the cholesterol, and deposits what is unused on the artery walls. This builds up into a plaque that narrows the arteries. HDL, the good cholesterol carrier, picks up this cholesterol and transports it back to the liver for reprocessing, and excretion from the body. Thus the proportion of HDL to LDL in the blood is important.

We can reduce our levels of LDL (bad cholesterol carrier) by eating fewer saturated fatty acids and cholesterol, found in egg yolks and animal and dairy fat. When this is coupled with a rise in HDL (good cholesterol carrier), it reduces the danger of suffering heart attacks, strokes and hypertension. By emphasizing fruits, vegetables, whole grains, and legumes in our diets, we help limit our intake of saturated fats and cholesterol, increase the proportion of HDL, and lower the amount of LDL in the blood. Table 8–A outlines how we can help control the types of cholesterol, raising or lowering the quantities in our bloodstream to emphasize the good carrier, and decrease the bad.

Table 8–A

HOW TO CONTROL THE TYPE OF CHOLESTEROL IN YOUR BLOOD	
To Raise HDL (good)	**To Lower LDL (bad)**
Engage in regular exercise	Engage in regular exercise
Don't smoke	Don't smoke
Use monounsaturated oils	Use monounsaturated oils
Reduce consumption of saturated fat	Reduce consumption of saturated fat
	Reduce consumption of cholesterol
	Use polyunsaturated oils

In most cases, the same activity raises the good cholesterol and reduces the bad. Conversely, when we consume saturated fat, smoke, and fail to exercise, we both lower our HDL (good) and raise our LDL (bad).

Function of fiber

New research confirms that fiber benefits our health. This indigestible part of our food is either water soluble or water insoluble. Water-soluble fibers dissolve in water and form a white paste that clears cholesterol from our bloodstream. It also helps regulate our blood sugar level following meals, thus reducing the serum insulin response, and preventing a plunge in our blood sugar level. Water-insoluble fibers create bulk in our intestines, improving regularity. They also protect against heart disease according to a 1996 Harvard University report, based on a six-year study of 44,000 middle-aged men.

Both types of fiber are found in rice, corn, oats, barley, legumes and unpeeled apples and pears. Table 8–B indicates the foods that provide either water-soluble or water-insoluble fibers.

Table 8–B

FOOD SOURCES FOR EACH TYPE OF FIBER

Water Soluble	Water Insoluble
Barley	Barley
Rice	Rice
Corn	Corn
Oats	Oats
Legumes	Legumes
Apples, peeled	Apples, unpeeled
Pears, peeled	Pears, unpeeled
Citrus fruits	Whole-wheat
Bananas	Root vegetables
Carrots	Leafy vegetables
Prunes	Strawberries
Cranberries	
Seeds	
Seaweed	

Some of the highest sources of fiber are cooked kidney beans, All Bran cereal, dried figs and prunes.

Nutritionists recommend 20–35 grams of fiber a day, derived from food, rather than fiber supplements. This eliminates the possibility of consuming too much fiber, which can cause us to lose nutrients, and experience digestive problems. They also recommend that we drink plenty of water to absorb the fiber.

How will I get sufficient protein?

"How do you get your protein?" people ask the vegetarian. Must of us grew up hearing we must be sure to eat adequate complete protein from meat, dairy products and eggs.

The great variety of protein molecules (and there are millions) are made from only twenty amino acids. The number and order of amino acids on a chain determine the type of protein molecule, whether it is hair, skin, or any other tissue. Of the twenty amino acids, eleven are made by our own body, while the remaining nine come from the foods we eat.

Where did the idea of the "complete protein" originate? Researchers, deciding that eggs were the perfect food, concluded that a "complete protein" must contain all nine of the amino acids not created by our body. Because many vegetables don't contain all nine "essential" amino acids, they were not considered a source of protein. Vegetarians were advised to properly combine grains with legumes, for example, in order to create a complete protein. One supplied the amino acids missing in the other. They also increased their consumption of eggs, dairy and soy products to ensure that they ingested adequate protein.

I wonder if humans could have survived in all their diversity, if getting adequate protein were indeed so involved. All proteins, regardless of their source, whether from other animals, plants, or our own bodies, are broken down in our bodies into their component amino acids. As almost all plants contain a variety of amino acids, they are an excellent source of protein. Studies confirm an earlier discovery of the amino acid pool in the body. When our body breaks down tissue that must be repaired or replaced, it recycles and stores the component amino acids that have just been released. The body combines these stored amino acids with the eleven amino acids that it makes and those from any food that is eaten to create the protein molecules it requires to maintain, repair and rebuild itself.

Happily for vegetarians, The American Dietetic Association, and different research studies, confirm that a varied nutritious diet of fruits, vegetables, whole grains, legumes, nuts and seeds provides all of the protein, carbohydrates and nutrients that the body requires. If we consume all the calories we require from a variety of wholesome foods, we will get adequate protein. Contrary to our prevalent fear of not getting adequate protein, most of us in the Western world consume far more protein than the body requires.

The question of calcium

Calcium, which is essential for strong teeth and bones, and the prevention of osteoporosis as we age, may be excreted from our body when we consume too much protein. Several studies indicate that vegetarians who also avoid caffeine and cigarettes, need to consume less calcium than people who eat meat. Vegetarians are also less likely to suffer from osteoporosis as they age. One study revealed that eighty-year-old vegetarian women had bones as dense as sixty-year-old meat-eating women.

Dairy products are not the only source of calcium. We may obtain it from tofu, beans, dark green vegetables, sesame seeds, and calcium-fortified products or supplements, as well as a variety of other foods.

But don't I need meat for strength and endurance?

Many of us believe we need meat, eggs and dairy products for strength and energy, and this may be your experience. Carnivores (meat eaters), however, sleep sixteen to eighteen hours a day. Body builders, who have traditionally eaten meat to get adequate protein, have been changing to a vegetarian diet. Studies indicate that vegetarians recover faster after exercise, and have more strength and endurance than those who eat meat. Stop and consider whether you feel more energetic and alert after eating soup and a salad, or after eating your traditional Thanksgiving dinner.

A combined study by scientists at Oregon State University in the United States and Charles University in Czechoslovakia shows that vegetarians have more "slow twitch" muscle fibers than people on a mixed meat and vegetable diet. Slow twitch muscle fibers, in contrast to fast twitch muscle fibers, are capable of greater endurance, and make better use of oxygen, which benefits the heart muscle.

Human anatomy and vegetarian diet

The human anatomy favors vegetarianism. Our teeth resemble those of the frugivors (fruit eating animals) — they are nearly all the same height, the canines are conical and blunt, and the molars are broad at the top with enamel folds. When we eat fruit alone on an empty stomach, it is digested quickly and effortlessly in about one-half hour. A study of the markings on the teeth of the earliest hominoids indicates they lived on fruits. A 1996 British research report from

Oxford University, based on a seventeen-year study of 11,000 adults over age 45, showed that eating fresh fruit daily significantly lowers the risk of dying before age 80 from heart disease and strokes.

Take advantage of these findings. Perform Exercise 8–1 and begin incorporating fruit into your diet.

Exercise 8–1   Begin to eat fruit daily

Beginning tomorrow, and for the next week, eat at least one serving of fruit every day. Enjoy it first thing in the morning on an empty stomach, when it will digest quickly and easily, and boost your blood sugar to start the day. At the end of the week, consider making this a daily habit. One serving is one medium apple or orange.

The carnivores (meat eaters) have canines which are long, smooth, and pointed for siezing their prey. Their molars are pointed and fit side by side to separate muscle fibers. Their stomach secretes twenty-five times as much hydrochloric acid as the human stomach, and their short digestive tract digests and eliminates the meat quickly.

Omnivores, such as bears, live on both plant and animal food. Their teeth are designed for this two-fold purpose, resembling both the herbivores/frugivores and carnivores.

Eating for health

The American Dietetic Association recommends 6–11 servings of grain products daily; 3–5 servings of green and yellow vegetables; and 2–3 servings of fruits each day. Servings are defined in Table 8–C below. While 6–11 servings of grains may sound excessive, a whole bagel is two servings, and only one-half cup of pasta constitutes a serving. Someone weighing about 110 pounds would eat 6 servings, while another weighing about 200 pounds would require 11 servings daily. Whole grains include whole-wheat, brown rice, oatmeal, millet, barley, rye, spelt, quoina (pronounced keen-wa), cornmeal, and more.

Table 8–C

American Dietetic Association
SERVING SUGGESTIONS FOR A HEALTHFUL DIET

*   2 – 3 servings of fresh fruits

*   3 – 5 servings of fresh vegetables

         1 serving is: 1 piece, such as 1 medium apple, carrot, or potato

                        1/2 cup cooked fruit or vegetable

                        1 cup raw, leafy vegetable

*   6 – 11 servings of grains, preferably whole grains

         1 serving is: 1 slice of bread

                        1/2 of a muffin or bagel

                        1/2 cup cooked pasta, rice, oatmeal, etc.

*   3 servings of nonfat or low-fat dairy products

         1 serving is: 8 oz. of milk or yogurt

                        1 oz. of nonfat cheese

*   2 servings of high-protein foods

         1 serving is: 1 cup of cooked beans, peas, lentils, (soy products)

                        3 oz. of fish, chicken without skin, extra-lean meat

---

While Table 8–C includes dairy products, fish, chicken and lean meat, as I mentioned at the end of the section about protein, in 1996 the American Dietetic Association confirmed that a plant-based diet provides everything the body requires.

Meat and dairy products contain saturated fat, as well as the hormones and antibiotics fed to the animals and poultry. If you include meat in your diet, you might try serving it only a few days a week. Instead of making it the main item on the menu, have it as part of a stir fry or casserole. If you eat dairy products, you can eliminate, or limit, the saturated fat by using the nonfat, or 1% fat variety, which derives 26% of its calories from fat.

Make a practice of reading the list of ingredients on canned and packaged food. It's wise to avoid products with numerous chemicals, preservatives, and artificial colors. The first ingredient on the list is the main one, followed by the others in descending order of quantity. When the list begins with salt, or sugar (including corn syrup, fructose, glucose, dextrose, honey and maple syrup), this is the main ingredient in the product. Sometimes there are several sources of sweetener in one package.

Notice what constitues a serving in each container, and how many servings it contains. Quantities of fat, sodium, fiber, etc. are listed per serving. We may eat more than one of their servings at one time, and must multiply quantities accordingly. Conversely, we may eat less than one of their servings. What are the total fat grams per serving, and how much of that is saturated fat? How much sodium does a serving contain? When I consider the quantities of fat, sodium, or sugar too high, I prefer to choose another product.

Consider shopping at food co-ops, natural food stores, and farmers' markets some of the time. You'll find some organic produce, and a variety of packaged products that may be lower in fat, salt, and preservatives.

Table 8–D

EASY WAYS TO INCLUDE FRESH FRUITS AND VEGETABLES IN YOUR DIET

- Eat one or two pieces of fruit while you get ready in the morning.
- At breakfast include juice, or sliced fruit on your cereal.
- Keep dried fruit, or fresh apples, bananas, or grapes in your desk, for snacks.
- Keep a bowl of fruit on a table at home.
- Prepare some carrot and celery sticks in advance. Include these in your lunch or use them as snacks.
- Eat lunch at a salad bar, selecting fresh vegetables. Limit pasta and potato salads as they are heavy on mayonnaise.
- Buy vegetables pre-cut, cleaned or shredded, if you don't have time to prepare them.
- Include several vegetables in your dinner menu.

Begin incorporating more fruits and vegetables into your diet with Exercise 8–2.

Exercise 8–2   Add more fruits and vegetables to your diet

Make an effort to follow some of the suggestions in Table 8–D. Begin by increasing the quantity of fruits and vegetables in your diet three days a week for a month. At the end of the month, increase the number of days per week that you eat these.

Incorporate simple vegetarian meals into your diet, by choosing some of the suggestions in Table 8–E.

Making the transition to a plant-based diet

We can make a gradual and effortless transition to a vegetarian diet. We might begin by eliminating red meat, limiting ourselves to poultry and fish. As time passes, we may choose to gradually eliminate the chicken and fish from our diet. In several months or years, we may decide to limit our consumption of eggs or dairy products, or to refrain from eating them entirely.

There are lacto-ovo vegetarians who eat no meat, but do consume dairy products and eggs. Lacto vegetarians eat dairy products, but don't include meat and eggs, and ovo vegetarians eat eggs, but avoid meat and dairy products. Vegans (pronounced Vee-guns) avoid all animal products, living on fruits, vegetables, grains, legumes, nuts and seeds. Dr. Barnard and Dr. Ornish recommend the vegan diet.

There are a large variety of good vegetarian cookbooks available. Peruse them before you buy. Make sure they include a variety of vegetables, legumes and whole grains, and that they don't rely heavily on dairy products and eggs. Be sure that the ingredients which predominate are those you enjoy, and that the recipes are as simple or complex as you desire.

You can begin the change to a vegetarian diet with the simple ideas found in Table 8–E, or intersperse more elaborate meals with these suggested foods. The simpler the better—for your health, ease of preparation, and clean-up.

When we eat natural foods in their natural state, we nourish the body, improve our health, minimize the time we spend in the kitchen, and increase the quality of our lives. At the same time, as noted in Chapter 9, we help the ecology and contribute to a more even distribution of the world's food supply.

Table 8–E

SIMPLE VEGETARIAN MEALS	

Breakfast: Fresh fruits and juices

Whole-grain cereals: cooked oatmeal – millet – rice or wheat farina –
flakes in cold cereals, preferably without added sugars
and fats

Whole-grain breads – muffins – bagels – scones

Nut butters – all fruit spreads

Lunch: Soups: lentil – split pea – bean – vegetable – tomato – minestrone

Sandwiches: Vegiburgers – avocado/cucumber/tomato/sprouts/lettuce–
bean spreads – nut butters

Salads: made with any combination of raw vegetables

Dinner: Stir-fried vegetables with brown rice or couscous. You may use tiny
amounts of water, or wine instead of oil, and cover with a lid to steam sauté,
instead of stir-frying in oil.

Baked potato (or rice or pasta) covered with sautéed onions, red peppers,
mushrooms, zucchini and broccoli

Mixed vegetable plate with a variety of steamed vegetables

Pasta with marinara sauce, vegetables and tofu

Pasta primavera: cooked pasta combined with several cooked
vegetables and tofu in a light salad dressing

Baked potato. Try it with ketchup, or topped with nonfat plain yogurt

Dessert: Fresh fruits – fruit cobblers – soy-or rice-based ice cream products

Snacks Carrot or celery sticks

Fresh fruit

Air-popped plain popcorn

Baked chips, low-fat

Nuts and seeds, preferably raw, unsalted (limit amount because high fat)

Crackers, low fat and low salt

Eating with awareness

We can increase our enjoyment of food, and help reduce the amount we eat, by eating with full awareness part of the time. Try eating one small bite with full awareness by performing Exercise 8–3.

Exercise 8–3   Eat a small bite of chocolate with awareness

Eat one bite of chocolate (or something else if you prefer) with full awareness. Slowly let the chocolate melt in your mouth, and savor the flavor. Don't eat any more. As the flavor fades, turn your attention to something else. What was your reaction to this experiment? Have you ever noticed that the first bite of food is always the most intense?

Adopt this practice with candy and dessert, if it appeals to you. You'll eliminate some fat and sugar from your diet without losing all of the pleasure. Reduce your consumption of other food by savoring it with full awareness. You may get as much delight as you usually do from "eating the whole thing," while distracted by conversation, your thoughts, or other activities such as reading or watching television.

Stay active to stay fit and healthy

"The evidence is indisputable now. As humans, we're at our healthiest when we're active," reports James M. Rippe, M.D., an associate professor of medicine at Tufts University School of Medicine in Boston. He cites over 100 major published studies relating to exercise and health, and, in particular, one which included 10,000 people. Those who were fit at the beginning of the study and remained so at the end had the lowest chance of dying from chronic disease. Those unfit at the beginning, but who became fit over a five-year period, reduced their risk by 44%. "The more fit you become," he states, "the more benefits you enjoy."

Benefits of weight training

Studies reveal that we lose 30% of our muscle mass between ages twenty and seventy. Much of this loss, however, is due to inactivity rather than simply aging. Nothing in our daily life gives us enough stimulation to build and maintain our muscle strength. The solution is weight training, which forces our muscles to work against resistance; and enables us to increase the size and strength of our muscle cells, regardless of our age. Researchers report that people in their eighties and nineties have doubled and tripled their strength after several months of strength training. It gives them more independence, as well as adding to the quality of their life. Individuals who begin strength training and other exercises during middle age, or younger, and maintain their exercise program, retain their vigor into their seventies and eighties.

By increasing our lean body mass, we increase our metabolic rate and burn more calories, even while our body is at rest. Thus we counteract middle-age spread, which is usually a gain in fat instead of muscle.

We can prevent or alleviate many of the aches and pains that we attribute to aging, by strengthening and stretching our bodies. Weight training strengthens muscles, tendons, ligaments and joints, which are then less injury prone. It improves flexibility, and it helps increase bone density and strength by minimizing the loss of bone minerals. Increased balance and coordination are other benefits we can enjoy. In addition to feeling increased health and vitality, we will look better as our muscles are toned and firmed.

Among other benefits, exercise reduces anxiety and raises our spirits. "The body is designed to release tension through exercise," according to Emmett E. Miller, M.D. Other studies confirm it.

The exercise pyramid

Experts suggest that just as we think of the four food group pyramid, we should think of a physical activity pyramid with several levels. The more of the levels we choose to include in our lives, the better, of course; but, we should try to make something from at least one of the levels part of daily life.

- At the broad base we include an accumulated thirty minutes of daily activities such as housework, yard-work, climbing stairs, and walking.

- At the next level up we should include twenty to sixty minutes of structured aerobic activity three to five times a week. This includes walking, jogging, swimming, cycling, or an aerobics class.

- Moving further up the pyramid, we find strength training with eight to twelve exercises covering all the major muscle groups. Performing eight to twelve repetitions for one to three sets, for each exercise, at least two times a week, will provide us with the weight training benefits previously mentioned. Experts recommend that we warm up with ten to twenty-five minutes of aerobic exercise such as cycling or walking, before a weight training session. Easy stretching exercises improve our flexibility. Fifteen to thirty seconds of steady stretch for each exercise will keep us limber, improve our posture, and reduce our risk of injury. Some of us stay motivated by joining and attending a health club. It's a good health investment. Others prefer to exercise at home, perhaps accompanied by one of the many exercise videos available.

- Recreational sports for fun or competition are at the top of the pyramid.

A study at the Cooper Institute for Aerobics Research has found that people who stroll at the rate of twenty minutes per mile, can achieve the same benefits of weight loss and cardiovascular protection as people who walk a twelve-minute mile, or jog a nine-minute mile. Consistency is the key—carrying out the activity consistently for a cumulative time period of two hours per week. Try a ten-to-thirty-minute walk before breakfast, perhaps while eating a piece of fruit, to enhance the way you feel for the rest of the day.

Begin to become more physically active by performing Exercise 8–4.

Exercise 8–4   Become more physically active

Choose an activity from one of the levels mentioned above, and perform it for the recommended time and intensity for one week. At the end of the week, add another week. Continue for one month. Find ways to stay motivated and to continue with your program.

Incorporate activities from other levels into your schedule as the months go by.

Summary of the benefits of physical activity

Physical activity ranks in importance with improved eating habits and nonsmoking for an active, healthful life. "Balanced fitness can do more to ensure a healthy, happy life than just about anything known to medical science today," according to Dr. Kenneth H. Cooper, founder of the Institute for Aerobics Research in Dallas, Texas, and world-renowned fitness expert. By beginning and maintaining a fitness program, we will reap large dividends both now and in the future. What more incentive do we need?

While most of the benefits may not be readily discernible, differences in muscle tone, posture, vitality, and zest for life are clearly visible when comparing active and inactive people. Benefits that are not so obvious include a lower incidence of: heart disease (by strengthening the heart muscle, and increasing the level of HDL, which clears cholesterol out of the bloodstream), hypertension, adult-onset diabetes, colon cancer, breast cancer, depression and anxiety. Other advantages include increased bone mineral content, muscle strength, balance and coordination, and improvement of the immune system.

More choices for better health

Other choices we can make to improve our health include:

- Drinking at least six 8-ounce glasses of water each day
- Refraining from smoking
- Limiting alcohol consumption
- Eliminating, or limiting, our caffeine consumption.

It is empowering to take responsibility for maintaining our health through lifestyle changes.

A growing number of people are also turning to alternative medicine to help maintain wellness, treat certain ailments, and limit their intake of drugs and antibiotics. The National Institute of Health has added a Department of Alternative Medicine to study the benefits of this growing trend. There are practitioners in acupuncture, herbal medicine, nutrition, naturopathic medicine, homeopathy, Ayurvedic medicine, massage and chiropractic. Their emphasis is usually on treating the whole person, and not simply on diagnosing and treating the symptoms of a disease or ailment.

Summary

We can improve our health and sense of well-being, and retard the physiological effects of aging, by emphasizing fruits, vegetables, whole grains, legumes, nuts and seeds in our diet; and making exercise a regular part of our lifestyles. By limiting our consumption of fat and emphasizing monounsaturated and polyunsaturated oils, we can help protect ourselves against certain cancers, heart disease, hypertension, strokes, cataracts, and diabetes. Research supports

The American Dietetic Association's finding that we get all the protein, carbohydrates, and nutrients we need from a varied, low-fat, vegetarian diet.

We are at our healthiest when we are active. Many problems attributed to aging are caused by inactivity, and can be alleviated by strengthening and stretching our bodies, and regular cardiovascular exercise.

Each one of us, of course, must choose the eating and exercise plans that meet his/her own needs and preferences. Consult your healthcare professional before you begin. As with the other aspects of simplifying life, simplifying our diet, and taking charge of our health and sense of well-being, involve greater awareness and self-responsibility. By incorporating a healthful eating and exercise plan into our lives through small weekly changes, we can enhance the quality of our health and improve the balance in our lives.

PROMOTING HEALTH

GOALS

Goal: Increase my consumption of fruits, vegetables, grains, and legumes

  Action: a) Consume 1–2 servings of fruit each day

  Consume 3–5 servings of vegetables each day

  Consume 6–11 servings of grains each day (preferably whole grains)

Goal: Limit my fat consumption

  Action: a) Stay below recommended 30% of calories from fat each day by:

  - Cutting back elsewhere, if I go over 30% in certain foods

  - Avoiding convenience foods with more than 30% of calories from fat

  - Limiting quantities of oil used each day in cooking, salad dressings, etc.

  b) Eliminate almost all saturated fat by:

  - Limiting my consumption of all animal products

  - Using nonfat or 1% fat dairy products

  - Limiting use of butter and margarine

  c) Use monounsaturated and polyunsaturated oils

Goal: Limit my sugar consumption

  Action: a) Limit use of sugar to two teaspoons daily

  b) Limit desserts or sweets to one small serving or less daily

  c) Limit soft drinks to one bottle, can, or less daily

Goal: Consume adequate calcium

  Action: a) Eat nonfat dairy products, green vegetables, tofu, calcium fortified cereals and drinks

  b) Take calcium supplement

  c) Don't consume excessive quantities of animal protein

Goal: Limit my salt intake

    Action: a) Avoid adding salt during cooking, or reduce amount used

                  b) Avoid adding salt at the table

Goal: Be aware of beverage consumption

    Action: a) Drink six or more 8-ounce glasses of water daily

                  b) Limit caffeine to two or fewer cups daily (coffee, tea, cola)

                  c) Limit alcohol to one serving or less daily

Goal: Consume adequate fiber

    Action: a) Obtain 20–35 grams of fiber from food sources daily

                  b) Consume both water-soluble and water-insoluble fiber

Goal: Include physical activity in my day. Choose one or more action steps that follow

    Action: a) 30 minutes daily of practical activity (housework, climbing stairs, walking)

                  b) 20–60 minutes, 3–5 times weekly, of structured aerobic activity (walking, jogging, cycling, swimming, aerobic class)

                  c) Strength training, 2–3 times weekly

                      8–12 exercises covering major muscles

                      8–12 repetitions for 1–3 sets, with 1 minute rest between sets

                  d) favorite recreational sports

Goal: Incorporate additional healthful habits into my life

    Action: a) Get adequate sleep

                  b) Have some time for relaxation

                  c) Refrain from smoking

                  d) Become an informed food shopper (read labels, limit processed foods)

                  e) Eat 3 meals a day, plus healthful snacks

CHAPTER *9*

LIVING MORE LIGHTLY ON THE PLANET

We are part of the earth and it is part of us

—*Chief Seattle*

The gift of simplicity is still an option on a planet barely capable of sustaining life as we presently know it. Scientists declare that if we do not make major changes in the not too distant future, we will no longer have a choice; a more stark existence will be forced upon us in a less than hospitable world.

The cost of the "good life"

We can no longer ignore the effect that our affluent lifestyle has on the destruction of the environment, and the quality of all life. Its impact is second only to that caused by the increase in world population. Continued economic growth is valued in Western societies, and planned obsolescence, high consumption, and widespread debt are taken for granted. However, the world's natural and mineral resources are limited.

The ozone layer, which is essential for protection from ultraviolet radiation, is being depleted by the emission of gases into the atmosphere. These gases cause air pollution and acid rain, which are harmful to people, forests and crops. Increasing quantities of carbon dioxide in the atmosphere, from burning fossil fuels and deforestation, are contributing to the threat of the greenhouse effect, global warming, and major climatic changes. The water supply is being polluted by pesticides, fertilizers, industrial waste, and toxic residue from commercial products.

Various aspects of the ecology are damaged by the massive quantities of waste generated in the Western world, particularly from food packaging.

The high price of meat

As compelling as the health reasons are for making the transition to a vegetarian diet, the impact of a plant-based diet on the well-being of the planet, and all of life, is even more dramatic.

Our planet's ability to provide food and energy is limited. The world's topsoil and pure water are disappearing. Almost 85% of the topsoil erosion in the United States is caused by overgrazing the rangelands, and the unsustainable farming practices used to grow crops. Over 50% of the crops raised in the United States feed cattle and other farm animals. Half of the water consumed is used to raise these crops, and provide drinking water for the livestock. Massive irrigation systems are depleting the ground water, which is being polluted along with the lakes and rivers, which carry eroded soil, waste from the livestock, and pesticides and fertilizers from growing their feed.

Rain forests are being destroyed to provide more rangeland, causing further soil erosion, and loss of habitat for countless species of plants and animals. It means less oxygen, and more carbon dioxide in the atmosphere. These losses are irreplaceable in our time.

Food production is seriously affected by the loss of fresh water and topsoil. Soil is blown away during droughts, and washed away in floods, in trampled and dried, overgrazed land. It is thought provoking to read in *Ecologue* that, "Twenty vegetarians can be fed on the amount of land needed to feed one meat-consuming person."

Simplicity is still an option

We can ask ourselves what we value more:

• Clean air and a protective ozone layer . . . or an automobile for every member of the family over sixteen years of age, in a growing population?

• Rain forests and dry forests to nourish all life, produce oxygen, regulate climate, and help prevent erosion . . . or the momentary financial reward from the sale of the timber, creation of more rangeland, and other short- term interests?

• Clean ground water, rivers and lakes, and irreplaceable topsoil . . . or meat on our plate every day?

Consider helping to reduce the waste in the landfills, and conserve natural resources by performing Exercise 9–1.

Exercise 9–1   Recycle to reduce waste in the landfills

Make recycling a daily habit by following the suggestions in Table 9–A. You will reduce waste in the landfills, and conserve natural resources.

Table 9–A

RECYCLE TO REDUCE WASTE AND CONSERVE RESOURCES

1) Recycle your usable clothing, tools, books, kitchenware, appliances, and furniture through charitable organizations, consignment shops, garage sales, and sales via classified ads.

1) Take part in your community's recycling programs. These usually include newspaper, brown paper bags, cardboard, scrap paper, glass, tin, aluminum, many plastic containers and bags.

1) Reuse glass jars and plastic containers to hold leftover food, freeze soups and other foods, and to store dry foods such as rice, beans, legumes, grains, pastas, nuts, cereals, and flours.

1) Reuse plastic bags when practical. Wash, rinse, and drip dry.

1) Use your own china mugs instead of Styrofoam, plastic, and paper cups, at your place of business, or where it is practical.

1) Reuse grocery bags, whether paper or plastic, or carry your own canvas or string bag to the store.

1) Eliminate, or limit, your use of disposable products such as razors, pens, and diapers.

1) Create gift tags from recycled Christmas cards, and other greeting cards.

1) Keep a rag bag and use old cloth rags to dust furniture, dry and polish the car, etc.

1) Buy recycled products.

1) Recycle at your place of business.

1) Encourage others to recycle, especially by your example.

1) Maintain a compost pile for organic waste, if you have some garden space.

1) Buy bulk food products to eliminate excess packaging.

1) Buy foods packaged in recyclable cardboard or paper, instead of Styrofoam and plastic.

Think about decreasing the amount of toxic residue being added to the environment by performing Exercise 9–2.

Exercise 9–2   Reduce toxic residue being added to the environment

Begin regular use of non-toxic products, or use some of the simple cleaning mixtures outlined in Table 9–B. You will be doing your part to decrease the amount of toxic residue going into the environment.

Table 9–B

SIMPLE NONTOXIC CLEANING MIXTURES

Produce Wash:	To remove oil-based chemicals: 1/4 cup white vinegar to 1 gallon water
	To wash off wax: mild solution of phosphate-free dish washing soap
General Cleaning:	Counters, floors, walls, rugs and upholstery: 1 quart warm water to 1 teaspoon each — liquid soap, Borax and vinegar. Keep in spray bottle for ready use.
Floors:	Vinyl: 1 quart water to 2 tablespoons vinegar. Damp mop.
	Wood: 1 quart water to 1 tablespoon liquid soap. Damp mop.
Glass:	1 quart water to 2 tablespoons vinegar. Use in spray bottle or in bucket, with cloth. Dry with old newspaper to eliminate streaks and lint.
Tub, Sink, Tile:	Sprinkle baking soda or Borax on wet rag. Rub. Rinse well.
Oven:	Sprinkle baking soda on spills when they're warm. Scrub off when cool. Use nylon scouring pad and wet baking soda to clean from time to time.
Mildew:	Baking soda or Borax on cloth. Scrub.
Polish:	Silver: Baking soda or toothpaste.
	Brass: Lemon juice.
	Copper: Lemon juice and salt
Drains:	If clogged, use plunger, or pour in 1/4 cup baking soda followed by 1/2 cup vinegar. Let fizz few minutes. Rinse with boiling water. Repeat if necessary. Don't allow hair or grease down drain.

The gift of simplicity

It is easy to feel that we, as individuals, are powerless to stop the widespread destruction of the environment. However, we are all responsible for the choices we make in our lives. As Duane Elgin writes, "The character of a whole society is the cumulative result of countless small actions, day in and day out, of millions of persons."

Our choices make a difference, and it is increasingly clear that as we give the gift of simplicity to ourselves, we give the gift of simplicity to all life, and to the planet.

Summary

The planet's natural and mineral resources are finite, and its ability to provide food and energy is limited. The world's topsoil and pure water are disappearing, as the water is polluted and depleted, and the soil eroded and lost through drought and flood.

The natural resources are further depleted by the high value placed on continual economic growth through planned obsolescence, and high consumption. The atmosphere and water supply are polluted by the emission of gases, waste generated by industry and food packaging, and toxic residue.

Simplicity is still an option, indeed a growing necessity. We can reduce our consumption, and conserve fuels, energy and natural resources. We can move toward a plant-based diet. We can recycle to reduce waste, and use nontoxic cleaners to reduce toxic residue. These are choices in favor of all life, and the planet we, and our descendants, must share.

LIVING MORE LIGHTLY ON THE PLANET

GOALS

Goal: Reduce demand for finite resources

> **Action:** a) Conserve water, oil, gasoline, electricity, natural gas
>
> b) Reduce high consumption
>
> c) Move toward a vegetarian diet
>
> d) Buy local produce to save energy used in transportation

Goal: Practice extensive recycling

> **Action:** a) Reuse glass and plastic containers
>
> b) Reuse paper and plastic bags
>
> c) Recycle newspaper, brown bags, tin, glass, aluminum, plastic, etc.
>
> d) Recycle usable clothing, tools, books, household items through charitable organizations, garage sales, consignment shops, ads
>
> e) Buy some recycled products
>
> f) Maintain a compost pile if possible

Goal: Reduce waste in the landfills

> **Action:** a) Limit purchase of disposable products
>
> b) Buy in bulk, when practical, to cut down on packaging
>
> c) Purchase products packaged in recyclable cardboard or paper

Goal: Limit addition of toxic residue to the environment

> **Action:** a) Buy nontoxic cleaners, or mix my own from suggestions in Table 9–B
>
> b) Grow some of my own produce, if possible, to reduce use of pesticides

Goal: Consider supporting an ecological organization

      Action: a) Donate my time and/or money

                        b) Support their activities and events

CONCLUSION

A simple life is its own reward

—George Santayana

When we review the choices, options, and opportunities we have discussed throughout this book, we find an underlying theme: With growing simplicity we enrich our personal lives, nourish our souls, and experience a growing sense of peace and inner connection. At the same time we are contributing to the health of the planet, and the quality of all life on the earth.

As we expand our awareness, and experience a greater sense of wholeness and inner connection, "old things will pass away." We will lose the desire for constant activity and endless acquisitions to relieve our restless longing, and fill our sense of emptiness. As our attitude toward possessions changes, we will experience a growing desire for the tranquility of uncluttered space, and the lightness and freedom of fewer possessions. By recycling our unused possessions, reducing our consumption, and maintaining what we own, we will reduce the need and the demand for many valuable resources.

By taking charge of our finances, asking ourselves if we really need another possession, and practicing delayed gratification to eliminate our debt, we will relieve our anxiety and increase our freedom. We will also decrease our demands on the world's natural resources.

As we move toward a vegetarian diet, we will improve our health, while making a positive impact on the earth's ecology. At the same time we will be contributing to a more equitable distribution of the world's food supply.

Whole and seamless as a circle, life invites us to enter wherever we find ourselves, and are ready to stretch and grow. As we develop our awareness, we will awaken in the months and years ahead. With growing perception and inner unfolding, we will gradually experience the joy and true fulfillment of inner completion.

APPENDIX

GENERAL GUIDELINES FOR PREPARING YOUR BUDGET

Income may come from one or several sources.

Fixed Expenses are often quite large, and must be paid at regular intervals. We should set aside funds for these expenses first. It is important to include a specific savings goal. Bank or invest that money when you are paid, or have it deducted automatically from your pay. In addition, build an emergency fund equal to three to six months living expenses, and keep it in a savings account, or other liquid form of investment. This will provide a cushion if you should be out of work for some time, or if you have an emergency repair or maintenance expense. It is important to replenish this fund again as soon as possible.

When you have entered the amounts for your fixed expenses, you can decide if economy measures are warranted. Perhaps you could reduce the number of your telephone services, change your method of transportation, or move to less expensive living accommodations.

Start a *Goals Worksheet* for future purchases. It will show you how much to set aside and save each month to reach these goals.

Changing Expenses vary from day to day and week to week. You will have more latitude to cut back and eliminate expenditures in these categories. Use your notebook record of daily expenses to determine the monthly totals on your worksheet for *Actual Changing Expenses*. Study them and decide where you can make some changes. Take into consideration the suggestions for saving in the finance chapter, your priorities, and the areas where you have decided to cut back in Exercise 6.5. Use a worksheet to make some calculations and reduce the amounts you have spent for such items as food, clothing, personal and entertainment expenses. Notice where your money is being spent thoughtlessly, and study your grocery receipts for modifications you can make.

INSTRUCTIONS FOR PREPARING YOUR BUDGET

Always use a pencil and eraser to work on your budget.

1) Determine your family's total *net income* for one month

    a) Record the amount you receive from each source of income

    b) Add the column to obtain your total net income

2) Calculate your *fixed expenses* for one month

    a) Enter the amount for your rent, or mortgage and real estate taxes

    b) Record your estimated utility bills, based on previous monthly statements

    c) Enter amounts for the remainder of your fixed expenses, based on previous statements, your checkbook, or other references

    d) Have a realistic monthly savings goal. Enter it. Divide among regular savings, specific goals, and emergency fund

    e) Total your fixed expenses for the month

3) Figure out your changing expenses for one month

    a) Use your record of actual expenditures from the notebook you carried for one month

    b) Total the amount spent in each category every day. For example, perhaps you purchased food in two stores on day (1). On the daily worksheet of actual changing expenses, enter the total for food under day (1)

    c) Follow the procedure in (b) for each day of the month. Total each column to get the month's actual changing expenses.

    d) Decide where you can cut back and make adjustments. In each category, allocate amounts that are realistic, and that will work for you.

    e) Enter the allocated monthly totals for each category on the changing expenses section of your budget

4) Balance the income and the total of both fixed and changing expenses.

    a) Income must equal total expenses

    b) If total income is greater than total expenses, decide where to allocate the extra funds; add them to savings, or to a category where you want to spend them.

    c) If total expenses are higher than income, decide where to cut back, and change the figures.

5) Keep a running total of your *actual expenses*, on a weekly basis.

    a) During your budget month, carry a small notebook and again keep track of every expenditure.

    b) At the end of the first week, total your expenditures, and enter them in each category for Week (1).

    c) When you conclude the second week, combine the total for Week (1) with the total for Week (2), and record this under Week (2).

    d) Continue this procedure for each week, to give you a weekly running total of *actual expenses*. Compare this with your budget at the end of each week, as you go through the month.

6) Strive to live within the budgeted expenses for the month.

    a) Cut back, do without, or postpone purchases, if the allocated amounts for any category are running out, or are spent before month's end.

    b) Congratulate yourself if you kept your expenditures within your budget for the month.

    c) Don't be discouraged if you exceeded your budget in some categories.

7) Prepare a new budget for the following month. This will be easier.

    a) *Income* and *fixed expenses* will be the same, or quite similar.

    b) You will have your cumulative weekly totals of *actual expenses* from the previous month to guide you.

    c) You can make further adjustments and refinements as necessary.

8) Prepare new budgets every month, and follow them, to successfully manage your money.

    a) The more you work with your budgets, the more realistic you will become, and the easier it will be to prepare and live within your budgets.

    b) The more you see the difference it can make to your life, the more you will want to simplify and save, and take control of your finances.

BUDGET FORMS

BUDGET for MONTH of _____	ACTUAL Cumulative CASH FLOW (a weekly running total)			
INCOME	Week 1	Week 2	Week 3	Week 4
Salary (net)	$	$	$	$
Social Security				
Pension				
Interest/Dividends				
Rental Property				
Child Support				
Alimony				
Other (bonus, gift				
tax refund,				
commission)				
Total Income				
FIXED EXPENSES				
Rent/Mortgage/Tax				
Electricity				
Gas				
Telephone				
Water/Sewage/Garb				
Insurance: Auto				
Health				
Life				
Homeowner				
Instlmnt: Credit Card				
Auto				
Other				
Savings				
Other				
Total Fixed Expenses				

		Week 1	Week 2	Week 3	Week 4
CHANGING EXPENSES					
Food	$	$	$	$	$
Clothing					
Transportation:					
Gasoline					
Car Maintenance					
Transit Fare					
Medical/Dental					
Dry Clean/Laundry					
Home Maintenance					
Personal:					
Hair Care					
Cosmetics					
Toiletries					
Cigarettes					
Other					
Entertainment:					
Movies/Concerts					
Books, Videos					
Dining Out					
Other					
Child Care					
Other:					
Contributions					
Allowances					
Travel, etc.					
Total Changing Exp.					

DAILY WORK SHEET OF ACTUAL CHANGING EXPENSES
MONTH _____

Day	Food	Clothing	Trans-port	Medical/ Dental	Clean/ Laundry	Home Maint.	Child Care	Other:
1								
2								
3								
4								
5								
6								
7								
8								
9								
10								
11								
12								
13								
14								
15								
16								
17								
18								
19								
20								
21								
22								
23								
24								
25								
26								
27								
28								
29								
30								
31								
TOTAL								

SUPPLEMENTARY WORKSHEET OF ACTUAL
PERSONAL & ENTERTAINMENT EXPENSES
MONTH _____

Day	Hair Care	Cos-metics	Toilet-ries	Cigar-ettes	Other	Movies, etc.	Books	Dining Out	Other
1									
2									
3									
4									
5									
6									
7									
8									
9									
10									
11									
12									
13									
14									
15									
16									
17									
18									
19									
20									
21									
22									
23									
24									
25									
26									
27									
28									
29									
30									
31									
TOTAL									

BIBLIOGRAPHY

Barclay, Florence. *The Mistress of Shenstone.* Grosset & Dunlap Publishers, New York, 1910.

Barnard, Neal D., M.D. *Foods that Fight Pain.* Harmony Books, New York, 1998. (Extensive resource list of scientific studies follows each chapter).

Braiker, Harriet B., Ph.D. *The Type E Woman.* Dodd, Mead & Company, New York 1986.

De Mello, Anthony. *Sadhana: A Way to God.* Image Books, Garden City, 1984.

Ecologue: The Environmental Catalogue and Consumer's Guide for a Safe Earth. Edited by Bruce N. Anderson. Prentice Hall, New York, 1990.

Elgin, Duane. *Voluntary Simplicity.* William Morrow, New York, 1981.

Foster, Richard J. *Freedom of Simplicity.* Harper & Row, San Francisco, 1981.

Goldstein, Joan & Soares, Manuela. *The Joy Within.* Prentice Hall Press, New York, 1990.

Harris, D. Mark. *Embracing the Earth: Choices for Environmentally Sound Living.* The Noble Press, Inc., Chicago, 1990.

Moyers, Bill. *Healing and the Mind.* Doubleday, New York, 1993. (Contains quotations from Jon Kabat-Zinn resulting from an interview).

Muller, Wayne. *Legacy of the Heart.* Simon & Schuster, New York, 1993.

Ornish, Dean, M.D. *Dr. Dean Ornish's Program for Reversing Heart Disease.* Random House, New York, 1990.

Peace Pilgrim: Her Life and Work in Her Own Words. Compiled by Friends of Peace Pilgrim, 43480 Cedar Avenue, Hemet, California 92544. An Ocean Tree Book, Santa Fe, NM, 1991.

Perkins-Reid, Marcia. *When 9 to 5 Isn't Enough.* Hay House, Carlsbad, CA, 1990.

Robbins, John. *Diet for a New America.* Stillpoint, Walpole, NH, 1987.

Sinetar, Marsha. *Do What You Love, The Money Will Follow.* Paulist Press, New York, 1986.

Thoreau, Henry D. *Walden.* First published 1854. Introduction and comments by Edwin Way Teale. Dodd, Mead & Company, New York, 1946.

Union of Concerned Scientists. *World Scientists Warning to Humanity.* 26 Church Street, Cambridge, MA 02238. December 1992. (Brochure).

The information in this book is offered to assist you in making some different choices for your life. Some programs, such as diet and exercise, will not provide the same results for everyone. You should consult your medical advisor to make sure you are in good health, and that any changes you undertake will not affect you adversely.

To purchase additional copies of this book

Electronic books may be purchased at www.1stbooks.com

Paperback (printed and bound) books may be purchased at www.1stbooks.com or ordered through Barnes & Noble, Borders, Amazon.com, or your favorite bookstore.

www.ingramcontent.com/pod-product-compliance
Lightning Source LLC
Chambersburg PA
CBHW081221280526
45787CB00006B/2468